DEPARTMENT OF THE NAVY
OFFICE OF THE SECRETARY
1000 NAVY PENTAGON
WASHINGTON DC 20350-1000

SECNAVINST 1752.4B
DON-SAPRO

AUG

I0438977

SECNAV INSTRUCTION 1752.4B

From: Secretary of the Navy

Subj: SEXUAL ASSAULT PREVENTION AND RESPONSE

Ref: See enclosure (1)

Encl: (1) References
       (2) Definitions
       (3) Responsibilities
       (4) Reporting Options and Sexual Assault Reporting
           Procedures
       (5) Commander and Management Sexual Assault Prevention
           and Response Procedures
       (6) Sexual Assault Response Coordinator and Sexual
           Assault Prevention and Response Victim Advocate
           Procedures
       (7) Healthcare Provider Procedures
       (8) Sexual Assault Forensic Exam Kit Collection and
           Preservation
       (9) Case Management for Unrestricted Reports of Sexual
           Assault
      (10) Training Requirements
      (11) Defense Sexual Assault Incident Database
      (12) Sexual Assault Annual and Quarterly Reporting
           Requirements

1. Purpose. This instruction updates policy and procedural
guidance for the Department of the Navy (DON) Sexual Assault
Prevention and Response (SAPR) Program, and implements
references (a) and (b).

2. Cancellation. SECNAVINST 1752.4A is hereby cancelled.

3. Definitions. See enclosure (2).

4. Applicability. This instruction applies to all
organizational entities of the DON and its two component
Military Services, the United States Navy and the United States
Marine Corps, including their Reserve Components.

a. Members of the following groups shall be provided full SAPR services and support, including Restricted and Unrestricted Reporting options:

(1) Service members of any Military Service who are on active duty and who have been sexually assaulted, regardless of when or where the sexual assault took place, including those who were victims of sexual assault prior to enlistment or commissioning.

(2) Reserve Component and National Guard members who were sexually assaulted while performing active service or inactive duty training.

(3) Military dependents, 18 years of age and older, who are eligible for treatment in the Military Healthcare System (MHS), and who were sexually assaulted by someone other than a spouse or intimate partner.

b. Reserve Component and National Guard members who were sexually assaulted while in civilian status (i.e., prior to or while not performing active service or inactive training) are only eligible to receive limited, immediate short-term SAPR support services from a Sexual Assault Response Coordinator (SARC) or Sexual Assault Prevention and Response Victim Advocate (SAPR VA), including Restricted and Unrestricted Reporting options. The SARC or SAPR VA will connect them to appropriate resources and service for further care and assistance.

c. Military dependents, 18 years of age and older, who were assaulted by a spouse or intimate partner, along with military dependents, 17 years of age and younger, who were sexually assaulted, are covered by the Family Advocacy Program (FAP). The installation SARC, the installation FAP, and domestic violence intervention and prevention staff shall coordinate when a sexual assault has occurred within a domestic relationship or involves child abuse.

d. Members of the following groups, who were sexually assaulted, are only eligible to receive limited SAPR support services from a SARC or SAPR VA while undergoing emergency care outside of the continental United States (OCONUS), and may only file an Unrestricted Report of sexual assault:

(1) <u>Department of Defense (DoD) civilian employees</u> and their family dependents, 18 years of age and older, who are stationed or performing duties OCONUS.

(2) U.S. citizen <u>DoD contractor personnel</u>, along with their U.S. citizen employees, who are authorized to accompany the Armed Forces in a contingency operation OCONUS.

e. Effective 31 August 2013, same-sex domestic partners of military members and, where applicable, children of the same-sex domestic partners, who are 18 years of age and older, and who were victims of sexual assault perpetrated by someone other than a spouse or intimate partner, and hold an Identification and Privilege Card (DD Form 1173) in accordance with DoD Manual 1000.13, Volume 1 "DoD Identification (ID) Cards: ID Card Life Cycle," August 31,2013, are eligible for the SAPR services of a SARC and SAPR VA, and limited emergency care medical services at a military Medical Treatment Facility (MTF), unless otherwise eligible for additional medical care in a military MTF. Same-sex domestic partners of military members and, where applicable children of the same-sex domestic partners, who are 18 years of age and older may file Unrestricted or Restricted reports of sexual assault (see reference (c)). Sexual assault that occurs within a domestic relationship or involves child abuse will be coordinated through FAP.

5. <u>Policy</u>

a. No form of sexual assault is ever acceptable anywhere in the DON. We seek a Department-wide culture of gender dignity and respect where sexual assault is completely eliminated and never tolerated, where sexual assault victims receive compassionate and coordinated support, and where offenders are held appropriately accountable. Every Sailor, Marine, and DON civilian shares dual responsibilities for their own actions and for protecting each other from harm. Our Core Values demand nothing less.

b. Combating sexual assault and supporting sexual assault victims are primary responsibilities at every level of civilian and military leadership. Commanders must take every report of sexual assault seriously, immediately refer reports to the Naval Criminal Investigative Service (NCIS) for investigation, support investigative and criminal justice procedures that enable persons to be held appropriately accountable, and actively protect sexual assault victims from retaliation or re-victimization. We seek to help sexual assault victims heal as individuals and succeed in their careers. Individuals who file an Unrestricted or Restricted Report of sexual assault must be protected from reprisal, or threat of reprisal, for filing a report.

    c. Victim-support SAPR services and medical care must be victim-centric, gender-responsive, culturally competent, and recovery-oriented. Sexual assault victims shall be given priority and treated as emergency cases. To the maximum extent possible, processes and terminology shall be standardized across Services and organizations. The establishment of performance standards for key victim-support processes, and their periodic structured assessment, are necessary for ensuring consistent and effective victim support.

    d. The SAPR program does not provide policy for legal processes within the responsibility of the Judge Advocate General (JAG) of the Navy or the Staff Judge Advocate to the Commandant of the Marine Corps (SJA to CMC) provided in the Uniform Code of Military Justice (UCMJ), the Manual for Courts-Martial, or for criminal investigative matters assigned to the DoD Inspector General, Naval Criminal Investigative Service, or other cognizant Military Criminal Investigative Organization.

6. <u>Responsibilities</u>. See enclosure (3).

7. <u>Records Management</u>. Records created as a result of this instruction, regardless of media and format, shall be managed in accordance with SECNAV Manual 5210.1 of January 2012. Those specific records associated with Restricted and Unrestricted Reports of sexual assault shall be managed in accordance with enclosure (4).

8. <u>Forms and Reports</u>

    a. "Initial Information for Victims and Witnesses of Crime" (DD Form 2701), available online at www.dtic.mil/whs/directives/infomgt/forms/eforms/dd2701.pdf.

    b. "Victim Reporting Preference Statement" (DD Form 2910), available online at www.sapr.mil/index.php/toolkit.

c. "DoD Sexual Assault Forensic Examination (SAFE) Report" (DD Form 2911) and associated instructions, available online at www.sapr.mil/index.php/toolkit.

d. "Military Protective Order" (DD Form 2873), available at www.dtic.mil/whs/directives/infomgt/forms/eforms/dd2873.pdf.

e. "Victim Advocate Supervisor Statement of Understanding" (DD Form 2909), available at www.sapr.mil/index.php/toolkit.

RAY MABUS

Distribution:
Electronic only, via Department of the Navy Issuances Web site
http://doni.documentservices.dla.mil

REFERENCES

(a) DoD Instruction 6495.02, "Sexual Assault Prevention and Response (SAPR) Program Procedures," 28 March 2013

(b) DoD Directive 6495.01, "Sexual Assault Prevention and Response (SAPR) Program," 23 January 2012

(c) Under Secretary of Defense for Personnel and Readiness Memorandum, "Changes to Department of Defense Issuances Regarding Benefits to Same-sex Domestic Partners of Military Members," 11 April 2013

(d) U.S. Department of Justice, Office on Violence Against Women, "A National Protocol for Sexual Assault Medical Forensic Examinations, Adults/Adolescents," current version

(e) DoD Instruction 5400.11-R, "Department of Defense Privacy Program," 14 May 2007

(f) Section 584 of Public Law 112-81, "National Defense Authorization Act for Fiscal Year 2012," 31 December 2011

(g) DoD Instruction 1030.2, "Victim and Witness Assistance Procedures," 4 June 2004

(h) SECNAV Instruction 5800.11B, "Victim Witness and Assistance Program (VWAP)," 5 January 2006

(i) SECNAV Instruction 7510.7F, "Department of the Navy Internal Audit," 27 December 2005

(j) Public Law 104-191, "Health Insurance Portability and Accountability Act of 1996," 21 August 1996

(k) DoD Instruction 6025.18-R, "DoD Health Information Privacy Regulation," 24 January 2003

(l) DoD Instruction 5505.18, "Investigation of Adult Sexual Assault in the Department of Defense," 25 January 2013

(m) Section 571 of Public Law 112-239, "National Defense Authorization Act for Fiscal Year 2013," 2 January 2013

(n) Directive Type Memorandum 12-004, "DoD Internal Information Collections," 24 April 2012

(o) Section 552 of title 5, United States Code, "The Freedom of Information Act," as amended

(p) Section 552a of title 5, United States Code, "The Privacy Act of 1974," as amended

DEFINITIONS

Unless otherwise noted, these terms and their definitions are for the purpose of this Instruction.

Collateral misconduct. Victim misconduct that might be in time, place, or circumstance associated with the victim's sexual assault incident. Collateral misconduct by the victim of a sexual assault is one of the most significant barriers to reporting assault because of the victim's fear of punishment. Some reported sexual assaults involve circumstances where the victim may have engaged in some form of misconduct (e.g., underage drinking or other related alcohol offenses, adultery, fraternization, or other violations of certain regulations or orders).

Confidential communications. Oral, written, or electronic communications of personally identifiable information (PII) concerning a sexual assault victim and the sexual assault incident provided by the victim to the Sexual Assault Response Coordinator (SARC), Sexual Assault Prevention and Response Victim Advocate (SAPR VA), or healthcare personnel in a Restricted Report. This confidential communication includes the victim's Sexual Assault Forensic Examination (SAFE) Kit and its information.

Consent. Words or overt acts indicating a freely given agreement to the sexual conduct at issue by a competent person. An expression of lack of consent through words or conduct means there is no consent. Lack of verbal or physical resistance or submission resulting from the accused's use of force, threat of force, or placing another person in fear does not constitute consent. A current or previous dating relationship or the manner of dress of the person involved with the accused in the sexual conduct at issue shall not constitute consent. There is no consent where the person is sleeping or incapacitated, such as due to age, alcohol or drugs, or mental incapacity.

Credible information. Information that, considering the source and nature of the information and the totality of the circumstances, is sufficiently believable to presume that the fact or facts in question are true.

Credible report. Either a written or verbal report made in support of an expedited transfer that is determined to have credible information.

Crisis intervention. Emergency non-clinical care aimed at assisting victims in alleviating potential negative consequences by providing safety assessments and connecting victims to needed resources. Either the SARC or SAPR VA will intervene as quickly as possible to assess the victim's safety and determine the needs of victims and connect them to appropriate referrals, as needed.

Culturally-competent care. Care that provides culturally and linguistically appropriate services.

Defense Sexual Assault Incident Database (DSAID). A Department of Defense (DoD) database that captures uniform data provided by the Military Services and maintains all sexual assault data collected by the Military Services. This database shall be a centralized, case-level database for the uniform collection of data regarding incidence of sexual assaults involving persons covered by reference (a). DSAID will include information when available, or when not limited by Restricted Reporting, or otherwise prohibited by law, about the nature of the assault, the victim, the offender, and the disposition of reports associated with the assault. DSAID shall be available to the DoD Sexual Assault Prevention and Response Office (SAPRO) and the DoD to develop and implement congressional reporting requirements. Unless authorized by law, or needed for internal DoD review or analysis, disclosure of data stored in DSAID will only be granted when disclosure is ordered by a military, Federal, or State judge or other officials or entities as required by a law or applicable U.S. international agreement.

Department of Defense (DoD) Safe Helpline. A crisis support service for victims of sexual assault in the DoD. The DoD Safe Helpline is available 24/7 worldwide with "click, call, or text" user options for anonymous and confidential support. It can be accessed by logging on to www.safehelpline.org or by calling 1-877-995-5247. It does not replace local base and installation SARC or SAPR VA contact information.

Designated activity. The agency that processes Permanent Change of Station (PCS) or Permanent Change of Activity/Assignment

(PCA) for expedited transfers. The designated activity for Navy is the Bureau of Naval Personnel. The designated activity for Marine Corps is Headquarters Marine Corps (HQMC) Sexual Assault Prevention and Response MFB to coordinate with the Deputy Director, Manpower Management (for active duty Marines) or the Branch Head, Reserve Affairs (for Active Reserve Marines).

Emergency. A situation that requires immediate intervention to prevent the loss of life, limb, sight, or body tissue to prevent undue suffering. Regardless of appearance, a sexual assault victim needs immediate medical intervention to prevent loss of life or undue suffering resulting from physical injuries internal or external, sexually transmitted infections, pregnancy, or psychological distress. Sexual assault victims shall be given priority as emergency cases regardless of evidence of physical injury.

Emergency care. Emergency medical care includes physical and emergency psychological medical services and a SAFE consistent with reference (d).

Final disposition. Actions taken to resolve the reported incident, document case outcome, and address the misconduct by the alleged perpetrator, as appropriate. It includes, but is not limited to military justice proceedings, non-judicial punishment, or administrative actions, including separation actions taken in response to the offense, whichever is the most serious action taken.

Gender-responsive care. Care that acknowledges and is sensitive to gender differences and gender-specific issues.

Healthcare personnel. Persons assisting or otherwise supporting healthcare providers in providing healthcare services (e.g., administrative personnel assigned to a military MTF). Includes all healthcare providers.

Healthcare provider. Those individuals who are employed or assigned as healthcare professionals, or are credentialed to provide healthcare services at a Medical Treatment Facility (MTF), or who provide such care at a deployed location or otherwise in an official capacity. This also includes military personnel, DoD civilian employees, and DoD contractors who provide healthcare at an occupational health clinic for DoD civilian employees or DoD contractor personnel. Healthcare providers may include, but are not limited to:

Licensed physicians practicing in the Military Healthcare System (MHS) with clinical privileges in obstetrics and gynecology, emergency medicine, family practice, internal medicine, pediatrics, urology, general medical officer, undersea medical officer, flight surgeon, or those having clinical privileges to perform pelvic examinations.

Licensed advanced practice registered nurses practicing in the MHS with clinical privileges in adult health, family health, midwifery, women's health, or those having clinical privileges to perform pelvic examinations.

Licensed physician assistants practicing in the MHS with clinical privileges in adult, family, women's health, or those having clinical privileges to perform pelvic examinations.

Licensed registered nurses practicing in the MHS who meet the requirements for performing a SAFE as determined by the local privileging authority. This additional capability shall be noted as a competency, not as a credential or privilege.

A psychologist, social worker or psychotherapist licensed and privileged to provide mental health care or other counseling services in a DoD or DoD-sponsored facility.

Installation. A base, camp, post, station, yard, center, homeport facility for any ship, or other activity under the jurisdiction of the Department of Defense, including any leased facility. It does not include any facility used primarily for civil works, rivers and harbors projects, flood control, or other projects not under the primary jurisdiction or control of the Department of Defense.

Installation commander. Commander of a base, camp, post, station, yard, center, homeport facility for any ship, or other activity under the jurisdiction of the Department of Defense, including any leased facility. It does not include any facility used primarily for civil works, rivers and harbors projects, flood control, or other projects not under the primary jurisdiction or control of the Department of Defense.

Non-Personally Identifiable Information (non-PII). Non-personally identifiable information includes those facts and circumstances surrounding the sexual assault incident or that information about the individual that enables the identity of the individual to remain anonymous. In contrast, personally identifiable information (see reference (e) for additional details) is information belonging to the victim and alleged assailant of a sexual assault that would disclose or have a tendency to disclose the person's identity.

Personally Identifiable Information (PII). Includes the person's name, other particularly identifying descriptions (e.g., physical characteristics or identity by position, rank, or organization), or other information about the person or the facts and circumstances involved that could reasonably be understood to identify the person (e.g., a female in a particular squadron or barracks when there is only one female assigned). See reference (e) for additional details.

Qualifying conviction. A State or Federal conviction, or a finding of guilty in a juvenile adjudication, for a felony crime of sexual assault and any general or special court-martial conviction for a UCMJ offense, which otherwise meets the elements of a crime of sexual assault, even though not classified as a felony or misdemeanor within the UCMJ. In addition, any offense that requires registration as a sex offender is a qualifying conviction.

Recovery-oriented care. Focus on the victim and on doing what is necessary and appropriate to support victim recovery, and also, if a Service member, to support that Service member to be fully mission capable and engaged.

Reprisal. Taking or threatening to take an unfavorable personnel action, or withholding or threatening to withhold a favorable personnel action, or any other act of retaliation, against a Service member for making, preparing, or receiving a communication.

Restricted reporting. Reporting option that allows sexual assault victims to confidentially disclose the assault to specified individuals (i.e., SARC, SAPR VA, or healthcare personnel), and receive medical treatment, including emergency care, counseling, and assignment of a SARC and SAPR VA, without triggering an investigation. The victim's report provided to healthcare personnel (including the information acquired from a SAFE Kit), SARCs, or SAPR VAs will NOT be reported to law enforcement or to the command to initiate the official investigative process unless the victim consents or an established EXCEPTION applies. The Restricted Reporting Program applies to Service members and their military dependents 18 years of age and older. Additional persons who may be entitled to Restricted Reporting are National Guard (NG) and Reserve Component members. DoD civilians and contractors, at this time, are only eligible to file an Unrestricted Report. Only a SARC, SAPR VA, or healthcare personnel may receive a Restricted Report, previously referred to as Confidential Reporting.

Sexual Assault Forensic Examination (SAFE) Kit. The medical and forensic examination of a sexual assault victim under circumstances and controlled procedures to ensure the physical examination process and the collection, handling, analysis, testing, and safekeeping of any bodily specimens and evidence meet the requirements necessary for use as evidence in criminal proceedings. The victim's SAFE Kit is treated as a confidential communication when conducted as part of a Restricted Report.

Sexual Assault Prevention and Response Office (SAPRO). Serves as the DoD's single point of authority, accountability, and oversight for the SAPR program, except for legal processes and criminal investigative matters that are the responsibility of the Judge Advocates General of the Military Departments and the IG, respectively.

Sexual Assault Prevention and Response Victim Advocate (SAPR VA). A person who, as a victim advocate, shall provide non-clinical crisis intervention, referral, and ongoing non-clinical support to adult sexual assault victims. Support will include providing information on available options and resources to victims. The SAPR VA, on behalf of the sexual assault victim, provides liaison assistance with other organizations and agencies on victim care matters and reports directly to the SARC when performing victim advocacy duties. Personnel who are interested in serving as a SAPR VA are encouraged to volunteer for this duty assignment.

Sexual Assault Response Coordinator (SARC). The single point of contact at an installation or within a geographic area who oversees sexual assault awareness, prevention, and response training; coordinates medical treatment, including emergency care, for victims of sexual assault; and tracks the services provided to a victim of sexual assault from the initial report through final disposition and resolution.

Sexual assault. Intentional sexual contact characterized by the use of force, threats, intimidation, or abuse of authority or when the victim does not or cannot consent. As used in this Instruction, the term includes a broad category of sexual offenses consisting of the following specific UCMJ offenses: rape, sexual assault, aggravated sexual contact, abusive sexual contact, forcible sodomy (forced oral or anal sex), or attempts to commit these offenses.

Unrestricted reporting. A process that an individual covered by this policy uses to disclose, without requesting confidentiality or Restricted Reporting, that he or she is the victim of a sexual assault. Under these circumstances, the victim's report provided to healthcare personnel, the SARC, a SAPR VA, command authorities, or other persons is reported to law enforcement and may be used to initiate the official investigative process.

Victim. Anyone who suffers direct physical, emotional, or pecuniary harm as a result of the commission of a sexual assault. For the purposes of this instruction, a person who asserts any such direct harm as a result of the commission of a sexual assault is presumed to be a victim. The term encompasses all persons 18 and over eligible to receive treatment in military medical treatment facilities; however, the Restricted Reporting Program applies to Service members and their military dependents 18 years of age and older.

RESPONSIBILITIES

1. <u>Director, Department of the Navy Sexual Assault Prevention and Response Office</u> (DON-SAPRO) shall:

a. <u>Department Representation</u>. Serve as the Department of the Navy representative to the DoD Sexual Assault Prevention and Response (SAPR) Integrated Process Team (IPT). Provide chairs or co-chairs for Working Integrated Product Teams (WIPTs) and representatives to DoD-SAPRO oversight teams when requested.

b. <u>Maintain Oversight</u>. Conduct site visits and other activity involving Navy and Marine Corps locations world-wide to maintain Secretariat visibility and oversight of Service-level SAPR programs and activities.

c. <u>Victim Support Performance Standards</u>. In coordination with Service representatives, identify at least four key milestones of Service-level sexual assault victim support processes and develop metrics for each suitable for quarterly reporting via DON-SAPRO to the Secretary. An initial plan shall be submitted to the Secretary within 90 days of the effective date for this Instruction. The first set of quarterly results for all four metrics shall be submitted to the Secretary within 180 days of the effective date of this Instruction.

2. <u>Chief of Naval Operations</u> (CNO) and <u>Commandant of the Marine Corps</u> (CMC) shall:

a. <u>Leadership Message</u>. Issue service-wide policy statements and utilize other available mechanisms to visibly promote a consistent top-down leadership message of gender respect, intolerance for sexual assault, and support for sexual assault victims.

b. <u>Guidance for Commanders</u>. Issue guidance for unit-level commanders to underscore their primary leadership responsibility for establishing command climates that discourage sexual assault, and for engaging responsibly in the management of alleged sexual assault incidents. Commanding officers must take each report of sexual assault seriously, immediately refer the allegation to Naval Criminal Investigative Service (NCIS) for investigation, support investigative and criminal justice procedures that enable persons to be held appropriately accountable, ensure that victims have access to SAPR support services and medical care, give conscious attention to protecting the victim from re-victimization or retaliation by the alleged offender or any others, and maintain awareness and engagement throughout the SAPR process.

    c. <u>Sexual Assault Prevention and Response Programs</u>. Ensure the operation of Service-wide SAPR programs for victim support in accordance with enclosures (4) through (12).

    (1) A 24-hour, 7-days-per-week sexual assault response capability for all locations, including deployed areas, shall be established for persons covered in this Instruction. An immediate, trained sexual assault response capability shall be available for each report of sexual assault in all locations, including in deployed locations.

    (2) SAPR services shall be gender-responsive, culturally competent, and recovery-oriented.

    (3) The terms Sexual Assault Response Coordinator (SARC) and Sexual Assault Prevention and Response Victim Advocate (SAPR VA) shall be used as standard terms throughout the Department of the Navy (DON) to facilitate communications and transparency regarding SAPR response capability.

    (4) All SARCs shall have direct and unimpeded contact and access to the installation commander for the purpose of this Instruction. If an installation has multiple SARCs on the installation, a Lead SARC shall be designated by the Service. For SARCs that operate within deployable commands that are not attached to an installation, they shall have access to the senior commander for the deployable command.

    (5) SARCs, SAPR VAs, and other responders will assist sexual assault victims regardless of Service affiliation.

    (6) At least one full-time SARC shall be assigned to each brigade or equivalent unit level of the Navy and Marine Corps (see reference (f)). Additional SARCs may serve on a full-time or part-time basis. Effective 1 October 2013, only members of the Armed Forces and civilian employees of the Department of Defense may be assigned to duty as a SARC.

(7) At least one full-time SAPR VA shall be assigned to each brigade or equivalent unit level of the Navy and Marine Corps (see reference (f)). Additional SAPR VAs may serve on a full-time or part-time basis. Effective 1 October 2013, only members of the Armed Forces and civilian employees of the Department of Defense may be assigned to duty as a SAPR VA.

d. <u>Training</u>. Ensure all military and civilian personnel receive SAPR training in accordance with enclosure (10).

e. <u>First Responders</u>. Establish and publicize policies and procedures for reporting a sexual assault.

(1) Require first responders to be identified upon their assignment and trained (see enclosure (10)), and require that their response times be continually monitored by their commanders to ensure timely response to reports of sexual assault.

(2) Ensure established response time is based on local conditions but reflects that sexual assault victims shall be treated as emergency cases.

f. <u>Victim Assistance</u>. Establish procedures that require, that each Service member who reports that he or she has been a victim of a sexual assault, upon seeking assistance from a SARC, SAPR VA, Military Criminal Investigative Organization (MCIO), the Victim Witness Assistance Program (VWAP), or trial counsel, be informed of and given the opportunity to:

(1) Consult with legal assistance counsel, and in cases where the victim may have been involved in collateral misconduct (see enclosure (2)), to consult with defense counsel.

(a) When the alleged perpetrator is the commander or in the victim's chain of command, such victims shall be informed of the opportunity to go outside the chain of command to report the offense, including to NCIS, another command, other commanding officers or an Inspector General, or other law enforcement officials. Victims shall be informed that they can also seek assistance from the DoD Safe Helpline.

(b) The victim shall be informed that legal assistance is optional and may be declined, in whole or in part, at any time.

(c) Commanders shall require that information and services concerning the investigation and prosecution be provided to victims in accordance with VWAP procedures.

(2) Have a SARC or SAPR VA present when law enforcement or defense counsel interviews the victim.

g. <u>Enlistment or Commissioning Waivers</u>. Ensure that individuals are not granted waivers for enlistment or commissioning in the Navy or Marine Corps when the person has a qualifying conviction (see enclosure (2)) for a crime of sexual assault or is required to be registered as a sex offender.

h. <u>Coordinating Office</u>. Identify a primary office to represent the Service in coordination of issues pertaining to sexual assault prevention and victim support with DON-SAPRO and other entities. This office shall coordinate with DON-SAPRO to identify at least four key milestones of Service-level sexual assault victim support processes, to develop metrics for each, and to provide quarterly results for reporting via DON-SAPRO to the Secretary.

i. <u>Budget Data</u>. Provide budget program and obligation data, as requested by DON-SAPRO.

j. <u>Research</u>. Provide DON-SAPRO a written description of any sexual assault related research projects contemporaneous with commencing the actual research. When requested, provide periodic updates on results and insights. Upon conclusion of such research, a summary of the findings will be provided to DON-SAPRO as soon as practicable.

k. <u>DoD Safe Helpline</u>. Establish procedures for supporting the DoD Safe Helpline in accordance with Memoranda of Understanding (MOUs) or Memoranda of Agreement (MOAs) between DoD-SAPRO and the DON, to include but not limited to, providing and updating SARC contact information for the referral DoD Safe Helpline database; providing timely response to victim feedback; and publicizing the DoD Safe Helpline to SARCs and Service members.

(1) Utilize the DoD Safe Helpline as the sole DoD hotline to provide crisis intervention, facilitate victim reporting through connection to the nearest SARC, and other resources as warranted.

(2) The DoD Safe Helpline does not replace local base and installation SARC or SAPR VA contact information.

l. <u>Reports to Combatant Commanders</u>. Require that reports of sexual assaults are provided to the Commanders of the Combatant Commands for their respective area of responsibility on a quarterly basis, or as requested.

3. <u>Chief, Bureau of Medicine and Surgery</u> (CHBUMED) shall:

a. <u>Training</u>. Ensure that all Department of the Navy (DON) military and civilian healthcare personnel, including those not assigned to Medical Treatment Facilities (MTFs), receive SAPR training in accordance with enclosure (10).

b. <u>Data Reporting</u>. Collect all data according to DoD annual reporting requirements, as explained in enclosure (12), and submit all data in coordination with Service inputs from the Navy and Marine Corps.

c. <u>Victim Care Protocols</u>. Ensure that all MTFs, along with deployable Navy and Marine Corps units with organic medical departments, have written gender-specific protocols for the management of sexual assault victims. At a minimum, protocols shall address all requirements for healthcare providers in enclosure (7), and applicable requirements for Sexual Assault Forensic Exam (SAFE) Kits in enclosure (8). All MTF protocols shall also address local procedures for providing access to SAFEs, and each MTF shall assign a healthcare provider as the primary point of contact concerning DoD, DON, and Military Service SAPR policy and for updates in sexual assault victim care.

d. <u>Sexual Assault Forensic Exams</u> (SAFEs). Ensure the implementation of ongoing training for healthcare personnel sufficient to maintain a broad-based capability to collect and preserve SAFE Kits.

(1) At a minimum, all MTFs with a 24/7 Emergency Room shall maintain an on-site capability to initiate SAFEs, along with SAFE Kit collection and preservation, within one hour of the procedure being requested by a credentialed healthcare provider or designated law enforcement official, as appropriate. In addition, protocols shall be developed and training instituted to ensure that chain-of-custody is maintained for SAFE Kits collected by any DON healthcare personnel.

(2) In the unusual circumstance where an MTF with a 24/7 Emergency Room is located in a civilian jurisdiction with an established network for conducting SAFE Kit collection in accordance with reference (d), and the MTF has assessed the standard of victim care in the established network and concluded a Memorandum of Understanding (MOU) or a Memorandum of Agreement (MOA) in accordance with enclosure (7), and where in addition the civilian jurisdiction has formally requested in writing that the MTF not conduct its own SAFE Kit collection, then the MTF may satisfy the above requirement by actively facilitating or providing victim transportation to the civilian network facility to ensure the victim arrives there within one hour of initial arrival at the MTF. The MTF shall also actively coordinate any appropriate follow-up medical care at the MTF itself.

e. <u>Coordinating Office</u>. Identify a primary office to represent Navy Medicine in coordination of issues pertaining to the medical management of sexual assault victims.

4. <u>Director, Naval Criminal Investigative Service</u> (NCIS) shall:

a. <u>Training</u>. Ensure that all NCIS military and civilian personnel receive SAPR training in accordance with enclosure (10).

b. <u>Data Reporting</u>. Collect all data according to DoD annual reporting requirements, as explained in enclosure (12), and submit all data in coordination with Service inputs from the Navy and Marine Corps.

c. <u>Case Review</u>. Develop quality standards for sexual assault investigations and establish an ongoing process for the timely review of all sexual assault investigations. Identify factors most strongly associated with victim cooperation or non-cooperation, and track the time to completion for all sexual assault investigations. Summary reports of findings shall be submitted to the Secretary, via DON-SAPRO, at least annually.

5. <u>Judge Advocate General (JAG) of the Navy</u> and <u>Staff Judge Advocate (SJA) to the Commandant of the Marine Corps</u> (CMC) shall:

    a. <u>Training</u>. Ensure that all military and civilian legal services personnel receive SAPR training in accordance with enclosure (10).

    b. <u>Data Reporting</u>. Collect all data according to DoD annual reporting requirements, as explained in enclosure (12), and submit all data in coordination with Service inputs from the Navy and Marine Corps.

    c. <u>Victim Assistance</u>.

        (1) Ensure that all members of the Navy and Marine Corps who are victims of sexual assault are informed of the availability of legal assistance provided by a military or civilian legal assistance counsel.

        (2) Ensure that all members of the Navy and Marine Corps who are victims of sexual assault are informed of their rights under the Victim Witness Assistance Program (VWAP), and that they receive a copy of "Initial Information for Victims and Witnesses of Crime" (DD Form 2701)(references (g) and (h)). In most cases, the completed "Initial Information for Victims and Witnesses of Crime" form (DD Form 2701) should be distributed to the victim in Unrestricted Reporting cases by DoD law enforcement agents.

        (3) Establish procedures to ensure that, in the case of a general or special court-martial involving a sexual assault (see enclosure (2)), a copy of the prepared record of the proceedings of the court-martial (not to include sealed materials, unless otherwise approved by the presiding military judge or appellate court) shall be given to the victim of the offense if the victim testified during the proceedings. The record of the proceedings (prepared in accordance with Service regulations) shall be provided without charge and as soon as the record is authenticated. The victim shall be notified of the opportunity to receive the record of the proceedings.

d. Supervise the Administration of Military Justice.
Conduct regular reviews of military justice training, manning,

processes, reporting, and accountability procedures. Identify
and disseminate best practices throughout the Navy and Marine
Corps legal communities.

6. Chief of Chaplains (COC) shall:

a. Training. Ensure that all chaplains and Religious
Program Specialists (RPs) receive SAPR training in accordance
with enclosure (10).

b. Data Reporting. Collect all data according to DoD
annual reporting requirements, as explained in enclosure (12),
and submit all data in coordination with Service inputs from the
Navy and Marine Corps.

7. Naval Inspector General (NAVINSGEN) and Deputy Naval
Inspector General for Marine Corps Matters (DNIGMC) shall:

a. Include specific assessments of SAPR programs in all
command inspections and area visits, and ensure that subordinate
inspectors general include SAPR program assessments in their own
unit-level inspection programs.

b. Provide copies of all findings relevant to SAPR programs
and sexual assault issues to DON-SAPRO.

8. Director, Naval Audit Service (NAVAUDSVC) shall:

a. Accept audit proposals for consideration from DON-SAPRO
on SAPR-related topics outside the normal Operational Planning
Board (OPB) process.

b. To the maximum extent possible under reference (i),
communicate with DON-SAPRO when planning SAPR-related audits, in
order to avoid redundant or conflicting efforts.

Enclosure (3)

REPORTING OPTIONS AND SEXUAL ASSAULT REPORTING PROCEDURES

1. <u>Reporting Options</u>. Victims of sexual assault, eligible under reference (a), have two reporting options: Unrestricted Reporting and Restricted Reporting. Unrestricted Reporting is favored by the Department of Defense (DoD) and the Department of the Navy (DON) because it improves the command's ability to support victims and enables criminal investigations. However, Unrestricted Reporting may inhibit some victims from accessing Sexual Assault Prevention and Response (SAPR) services and medical care when they do not want their command or law enforcement to be involved. In that circumstance, Restricted Reporting provides victims with an alternative and confidential disclosure option. For both Restricted and Unrestricted Reporting, the confidentiality of medical information shall be maintained.

a. <u>Unrestricted Reporting</u>. This reporting option triggers an investigation and Command notification, and allows a person who has been sexually assaulted to access medical treatment and counseling. When a sexual assault is reported through Unrestricted Reporting, a Sexual Assault Response Coordinator (SARC) shall be notified, who shall in turn either respond or direct a Sexual Assault Prevention and Response Victim Advocate (SAPR VA) to respond, assign a SAPR VA, and offer the victim healthcare treatment and a Sexual Assault Forensic Exam (SAFE). A completed "Initial Information for Victims and Witnesses of Crime" form (DD Form 2701), which sets out victims' rights and points of contact, shall be distributed to the victim in Unrestricted Reporting cases by Naval Criminal Investigative Service (NCIS) or other DoD law enforcement agents. If a victim elects this reporting option, a victim may not change from an Unrestricted to a Restricted Report. Information regarding Unrestricted Reports shall only be released to personnel with an official need to know or as authorized by law.

b. <u>Restricted Reporting</u>. This reporting option does NOT trigger an investigation. The commander/installation commander is notified that "an alleged sexual assault" occurred, but is not given the victim's name or other Personally Identifiable Information (PII). Restricted Reporting allows Service members and military dependents who are adult sexual assault victims to confidentially disclose the assault to specified individuals

(SARC, SAPR VA, or healthcare personnel) and receive healthcare treatment and the assignment of a SARC and SAPR VA. When a sexual assault is reported through Restricted Reporting, a SARC shall be notified, respond or direct a SAPR VA to respond, assign a SAPR VA, and offer the victim healthcare treatment and a SAFE. The Restricted Reporting option is only available to Service members and adult military dependents. Restricted Reporting may not remain an option in a jurisdiction that requires mandatory reporting, or if a victim first reports to a civilian facility or civilian authority, which will vary by State, territory, and oversees agreements. If a victim elects this reporting option, a victim may change from Restricted Report to an Unrestricted Report at any time.

(1) Only the SARC, SAPR VA, and healthcare personnel are designated as authorized to accept a Restricted Report. Healthcare personnel, to include psychotherapists and other personnel listed in Military Rule of Evidence (MRE) 513, who received a Restricted Report shall immediately call a SARC or SAPR VA to assure that a victim is offered SAPR services and so that a "Victim Reporting Preference Statement" (DD Form 2910) can be completed.

(2) A SAFE and the information contained in its accompanying Kit are provided the same confidentiality as is afforded victim statements under the Restricted Reporting option (see enclosure (8)).

(3) Chaplains and legal assistance attorneys have separate bases of privileged communications from SARCs and SAPR VAs, and neither chaplains nor legal assistance attorneys can accept a Restricted Report. In the course of otherwise privileged communications with a chaplain or legal assistance attorney, a victim may indicate that he or she wishes to file a Restricted Report. If this occurs, a chaplain and legal assistance attorney shall facilitate contact with a SARC or SAPR VA to ensure that a victim is offered SAPR services and so that a DD Form 2910 can be completed.

(4) A victim has a privilege to refuse to disclose and to prevent any other person from disclosing a confidential communication between a victim and a victim advocate, in a case arising under the Uniform Code of Military Justice (UCMJ), if

such communication is made for the purpose of facilitating advice or supportive assistance to the victim.

(5) A sexual assault victim certified under the Personnel Reliability Program (PRP) is eligible for both the Restricted and Unrestricted reporting options. If electing Restricted Reporting, the victim is required to advise the competent medical authority of any factors that could have an adverse impact on the victim's performance, reliability, or safety while performing PRP duties. If necessary, the competent medical authority will inform the certifying official that the person in question should be temporarily suspended from PRP status, without revealing that the person is a victim of sexual assault, thus preserving the Restricted Report.

c. Non-Participating Victim. A non-participating victim is a victim choosing not to participate in the military justice system. For victims choosing either Restricted or Unrestricted Reporting, the following guidelines apply:

(1) Details regarding the incident will be limited to only those personnel who have an official need to know. The victim's decision to decline to participate in an investigation or prosecution should be honored by all personnel charged with the investigation and prosecution of sexual assault cases, including, but not limited to, commanders, DoD law enforcement officials, and personnel in the victim's chain of command. If at any time the victim who originally chose the Unrestricted Reporting option declines to participate in an investigation or prosecution, that decision should be honored in accordance with this subparagraph. However, the victim cannot change from an Unrestricted to a Restricted Report. The victim should be informed by the SARC or SAPR VA that the investigation may continue regardless of whether the victim participates.

(2) The victim's decision not to participate in an investigation or prosecution will not affect access to SARC and SAPR VA services or medical and psychological care. These services shall be made available to all eligible sexual assault victims.

(3) If a victim approaches a SARC and SAPR VA and begins to make a report, but then changes his or her mind and leaves without signing the DD Form 2910 (where the reporting option is

selected), the SARC or SAPR VA is not under any obligation or duty to inform investigators or commanders about this report and will not produce the report or disclose the communications surrounding the report. If commanders or law enforcement ask about the report, disclosures can only be made in accordance with exceptions to Military Rule of Evidence (MRE) 514 privilege.

    d. Disclosure of Confidential Communications. In cases where a victim elects Restricted Reporting, the SARC, SAPR VA, and healthcare personnel may not disclose confidential communications or the SAFE and the accompanying Kit to DoD law enforcement or command authorities, either within or outside the DoD, except as provided in this Instruction. In certain situations, information about a sexual assault may come to the commander's or DoD law enforcement official's (to include Military Criminal Investigative Organizations (MCIOs)) attention from a source independent of the Restricted Reporting avenues and an independent investigation is initiated. In these cases, SARCs, SAPR VAs, and healthcare personnel are prevented from disclosing confidential communications under Restricted Reporting, unless an exception applies. Improper disclosure of confidential communications or improper release of medical information are prohibited under the provisions of the Health Insurance Portability and Accountability Act (HIPAA) (reference (j)) and the DoD Health Information Privacy Regulation (reference (k)) and may result in disciplinary action pursuant to the Uniform Code of Military Justice (UCMJ) or other adverse personnel or administrative actions. Even proper release of Restricted Reporting information should be limited to those with an official need to know or as authorized by law.

    e. Victim Confiding in Another Person. In establishing the Restricted Reporting option, DoD recognizes that a victim may tell someone (e.g., roommate, friend, family member) that a sexual assault has occurred before considering whether to file a Restricted or Unrestricted Report.

    (1) A victim's communication with another person (e.g., roommate, friend, family member) does not, in and of itself, prevent the victim from later electing to make a Restricted Report. Restricted Reporting is confidential, not anonymous, reporting. However, if the person to whom the victim confided the information (e.g., roommate, friend, family member) is in

the victim's officer and non-commissioned officer chain of command or DoD law enforcement, there can be no Restricted Report.

(2) Communications between the victim and a person other than the SARC, SAPR VA, or healthcare personnel are NOT confidential and do not receive the protections of Restricted Reporting.

f. <u>Independent Investigations</u>. Independent investigations are not initiated by the victim. If information about a sexual assault comes to a commander's attention from a source other than a victim who has elected Restricted Reporting or where no election has been made by the victim, that commander shall report the matter to an MCIO and an official (independent) investigation may be initiated based on that independently acquired information.

(1) If there is an ongoing independent investigation, the sexual assault victim will no longer have the option of Restricted Reporting when:

(a) DoD law enforcement informs the SARC of the investigation, and

(b) The victim has not already elected Restricted Reporting.

(2) The timing of filing a Restricted Report is crucial. The victim MUST take advantage of the Restricted Reporting option BEFORE the SARC is informed of the investigation. The SARC then shall inform the victim of an ongoing independent investigation of the sexual assault. If an independent investigation begins AFTER the victim has formally elected Restricted Reporting, the independent investigation has NO impact on the victim's Restricted Report and the victim's communications and SAFE Kit remain confidential, to the extent authorized by law.

g. <u>Mandatory Reporting Laws and Cases Investigated by Civilian Law Enforcement</u>. Health care may be provided and SAFE Kits may be performed in a jurisdiction bound by State and local laws that require certain personnel (usually health care personnel) to report the sexual assault to civilian agencies or law enforcement. In some cases, civilian law enforcement may take jurisdiction of the sexual assault case, or the civilian jurisdiction may inform the military law enforcement or investigative community of a sexual assault that was reported to it. In such instances, it may not be possible for a victim to make a Restricted Report or it may not be possible to maintain the report as a Restricted Report. To the extent possible, DoD will honor the Restricted Report; however, sexual assault victims need to be aware that their Restricted Report is not guaranteed due to circumstances surrounding the independent investigation and requirements of individual State laws. In order to take advantage of the Restricted Reporting option, the victim must file a restricted report BEFORE the SARC is informed of an ongoing independent investigation of the sexual assault.

2. <u>Initiating Medical Care and Treatment upon Receipt of Report</u>. Healthcare personnel will initiate the emergency care and treatment of sexual assault victims and notify the SARC or the SAPR VA (see enclosure (7)). Upon receipt of a Restricted Report, only the SARC or the SAPR VA will be notified. There will be NO report to DoD law enforcement, a supervisory official, or the victim's chain of command by the healthcare personnel, unless an exception to Restricted Reporting applies or applicable law requires other officials to be notified. Regardless of whether the victim elects Restricted or Unrestricted Reporting, confidentiality of medical information will be maintained in accordance with applicable laws and regulations.

3. <u>Reports and Commanders</u>

    a. <u>Unrestricted Reports to Commanders</u>. The SARC shall provide the installation commander of sexual assault victims with information regarding all Unrestricted Reports within 24 hours of an Unrestricted Report of sexual assault. This notification may be extended by the commander to 48 hours after the Unrestricted Report of the incident when there are extenuating circumstances in deployed environments.

    b. <u>Restricted Reports to Commanders</u>. For the purposes of public safety and command responsibility, in the event of a Restricted Report, the SARC shall report non-PII concerning sexual assault incidents (without information that could reasonably lead to personal identification of the victim or the alleged assailant to only the commander/installation commander within 24 hours of the report. This notification may be extended by the commander to 48 hours after the Restricted Report of the incident when there are extenuating circumstances in deployed environments. The SARC's communications with victims are protected by the Restricted Reporting option and MRE 514.

(1) Even if the victim chooses not to pursue an investigation, Restricted Reporting gives the installation commander a clearer picture of the reported sexual assaults within the command. The installation commander can then use the information to enhance preventive measures, to enhance the education and training of the command's personnel, and to scrutinize more closely the organization's climate and culture for contributing factors.

(2) Neither the installation commander nor DoD law enforcement may use the information from a Restricted Report for investigative purposes or in a manner that is likely to discover, disclose, or reveal the identities of the victims unless an exception applies (see paragraph 4(b) below). Improper disclosure of Restricted Reporting information may result in discipline pursuant to the UCMJ or other adverse personnel or administrative actions.

4. Exceptions to Restricted Reporting and Disclosures

a. The SARC will evaluate the confidential information provided under the Restricted Report to determine whether an exception applies.

(1) The SARC shall disclose the otherwise protected confidential information only after consultation with the Staff Judge Advocate (SJA) of the installation commander, supporting judge advocate or other legal advisor concerned, who shall advise the SARC whether an exception to Restricted Reporting applies. In addition, the SJA, supporting judge advocate, or other legal advisor concerned will analyze the impact of MRE 514 on the communications.

(2) When there is uncertainty or disagreement on whether an exception to Restricted Reporting applies, the matter shall be brought to the attention of the installation commander for decision without identifying the victim (using non-PII information). Improper disclosure of confidential communications under Restricted Reporting, improper release of medical information, and other violations of this guidance are prohibited and may result in discipline pursuant to the UCMJ or State statute, loss of privileges, loss of certification or credentialing, or other adverse personnel or administrative actions.

b. The following exceptions to the prohibition against disclosures of Restricted Reporting authorize a disclosure of a Restricted Report only if one or more of the following conditions apply:

(1) Authorized by the victim in writing.

(2) Necessary to prevent or mitigate a serious and imminent threat to the health or safety of the victim or another person; for example, multiple reports involving the same alleged suspect (repeat offender) could meet this criteria.

(3) Required for fitness for duty or disability determinations. This disclosure is limited to only the information necessary to process duty or disability determinations for Service members.

(4) Required for the supervision of coordination of direct victim treatment or services. The SARC, SAPR VA, or healthcare personnel can disclose specifically requested information to those individuals with an official need to know, or as required by law or regulation.

(5) Ordered by a military official (e.g., a duly authorized trial counsel subpoena in a UCMJ case), Federal or State judge, or as required by a Federal or State statute or applicable U.S. international agreement. The SARC, SAPR VA, and healthcare personnel will consult with the installation commander's servicing legal office, in the same manner as other recipients of privileged information, to determine if the exception criteria apply and whether a duty to disclose the

otherwise protected information is present. Until those determinations are made, only non-PII shall be disclosed.

c. Healthcare personnel may also convey to the victim's unit commander any possible adverse duty impact related to the victim's medical condition and prognosis. However, such circumstances do NOT otherwise warrant a Restricted Reporting exception to policy. Therefore, the confidential communication related to the sexual assault may not be disclosed. Improper disclosure of confidential communications, improper release of medical information, and other violations of this Instruction are prohibited and may result in discipline pursuant to the UCMJ or State statute, loss of privileges, or other adverse personnel or administrative actions.

d. The SARC or SAPR VA shall inform the victim when a disclosure in accordance with the exceptions in this section of this enclosure is made.

e. If a SARC, SAPR VA, or healthcare personnel make an unauthorized disclosure of a confidential communication, that person is subject to disciplinary action. Unauthorized disclosure has no impact on the status of the Restricted Report. All Restricted Reporting information is still confidential and protected. However, unauthorized or inadvertent disclosures made to a commander or law enforcement shall result in notification to the MCIO.

5. Actionable Rights. Restricted Reporting does not create any actionable rights for the victim or alleged offender or constitute a grant of immunity for any actionable conduct by the offender or the victim.

6. Document Retention. Each Service will have two separate document retention schedules for records of Service members who report that they are victims of sexual assault, based on whether the Service member filed a Restricted or Unrestricted Report. The record retention system for Restricted Reports shall protect the Service member's desire for confidentiality.

a. Document Retention for Unrestricted Reports:

(1) The SARC will enter the Unrestricted Report DD Form 2910 in the Defense Sexual Assault Incident Database (DSAID)

system as an electronic record, where it will be retained for 50 years from the date the victim signed the DD Form 2910.

(2) The "DoD Sexual Assault Forensic Examination (SAFE) Report" (DD Form 2911) shall be retained in accordance with DoD Instruction 5505.18 (reference (l)).

b. Document Retention for Restricted Reports:

(1) The SARC will retain a hard copy of the Restricted Report DD Form 2910 for 5 years, in a manner consistent with DoD requirements for the secure storage of PII (see reference (e)). The 5-year time frame for the DD Form 2910 will start from the date the victim signs the DD Form 2910. However, at the request of a Service member who files a Restricted Report on an incident of sexual assault, the DD Forms 2910 and 2911 filed in connection with the Restricted Report will be retained for 50 years.

(2) The SAFE Kit, which includes the DD Form 2911 or civilian forensic examination report, if available, will be retained for 5 years in a location designated by the Military Service concerned. The 5-year time frame will start from the date the victim signs the DD Form 2910.

COMMANDER AND MANAGEMENT
SEXUAL ASSAULT PREVENTION AND RESPONSE
PROCEDURES

1. <u>Sexual Assault Prevention and Response (SAPR) Management</u>.
Commanders, supervisors, and managers at all levels are
responsible for the effective implementation of the SAPR program
and policy. Military and Department of Defense (DoD) civilian
officials at each management level shall advocate a strong SAPR
program and provide education and training that shall enable
them to prevent and appropriately respond to incidents of sexual
assault.

2. <u>Installation Commander SAPR Response Procedures</u>. Each
installation commander shall develop guidelines to establish a
24-hour, 7-days-per-week sexual assault response capability for
their locations, including deployed areas. The Sexual Assault
Response Coordinator (SARC) or a Sexual Assault Prevention and
Response Victim Advocate (SAPR VA) shall be immediately called
in every reported incident of sexual assault on a military
installation. For SARCs that operate within deployable commands
that are not attached to an installation, senior commanders of
the deployable commands shall ensure that equivalent SAPR
standards are met.

3. <u>Commander SAPR Response Procedures</u>. Each Commander shall:

   a. Encourage the use of the commander's sexual assault
response protocols for Unrestricted Reports as the baseline for
commander's response to the victim, an offender, and proper
response of a sexual assault within a unit. The Commander's
Sexual Assault Response Protocols for Unrestricted Reports of
Sexual Assault are located in the SAPR Policy Toolkit, on
www.sapr.mil. These protocols may be expanded to meet Military
Service-specific requirements and procedures.

   b. Meet with the SARC within 30 days of taking command for
one-on-one SAPR training. The training shall include a trends
brief for unit and area of responsibility and the
confidentiality requirements in Restricted Reporting. The
commander must contact the judge advocate for training on the
Military Rule of Evidence (MRE) 514 privilege.

   c. Require the SARC to:

(1) Be notified of every incident of sexual assault involving Service members or persons covered in this Instruction, in or outside of the military installation when reported to DoD personnel. When notified, the SARC or SAPR VA shall respond to offer the victim SAPR services. All SARCs shall be authorized to perform victim advocate duties in accordance with service regulations, and will be acting in the performance of those duties.

      (a) In Restricted Reports, the SARC shall be notified by the healthcare personnel or the SAPR VA.

      (b) In Unrestricted Reports, the SARC shall be notified by the DoD responders.

(2) Provide the installation commander with information regarding an Unrestricted Report within 24 hours of an Unrestricted Report of sexual assault.

(3) Provide the installation commander with non-Personally Identifiable Information (non-PII) within 24 hours of a Restricted Report of sexual assault. This notification may be extended to 48 hours after the report of the incident if there are extenuating circumstances in the deployed environment. Command and installation demographics shall be taken into account when determining the information to be provided.

(4) Be supervised and evaluated by the installation commander or deputy installation commander in the performance of SAPR procedures in accordance with enclosure (6).

(5) Receive SARC training to follow procedures in accordance with enclosure (6). In accordance with the DoD Sexual Assault Advocate Certification Program (D-SAACP), standardized criteria for the selection and training of SARCs and SAPR VAs shall comply with specific Military Service guidelines and certification requirements, when implemented by the Department of Defense Sexual Assault Prevention and Response Office (DoD-SAPRO).

(6) Follow established procedures to store the "Victim Reporting Preference Statement" (DD Form 2910) pursuant to Military Service regulations regarding the storage of documents with PII. Follow established procedures to store the original

DD Form 2910 and ensure that all Federal and Service privacy regulations are adhered to.

d. Evaluate medical personnel per Department of the Navy and Military Service regulations in the performance of SAPR procedures as described in enclosure (7).

e. Require adequate supplies of Sexual Assault Forensic Exam (SAFE) Kits be maintained in all locations where SAFEs are conducted, including deployed locations. The supplies shall be routinely evaluated to guarantee adequate numbers to meet the need of sexual assault victims. Military Service SAPR personnel, to include medical personnel, shall be appropriately trained on protocols for the use of the SAFE kit.

f. Require DoD law enforcement and healthcare personnel to comply with prescribed chain of custody procedures described in their Military Service-specific Military Criminal Investigative Organization (MCIO) procedures. Modified procedures applicable in cases of Restricted Reports of sexual assault are explained in enclosure (8).

g. Require that a Case Management Group (CMG) is conducted on a monthly basis in accordance with enclosure (9).

(1) Chair (if the Installation Commander or Deputy Installation Commander) or attend the CMG, as appropriate. Direct the required CMG members to attend.

(2) Commanders shall provide victims of a sexual assault who filed an Unrestricted Reports monthly updates regarding the current status of any ongoing investigative, medical, legal, or command proceedings regarding the sexual assault until the final disposition of the reported assault. This is a non-delegable commander duty. This update must occur within 72 hours of the last CMC.

h. Ensure that resolution of Unrestricted Report sexual assault cases shall be expedited.

(1) A unit commander who receives an Unrestricted Report of a sexual assault shall immediately refer the matter to the Naval Criminal Investigative Service (NCIS) or appropriate MCIO, regardless of the severity of the allegation, offense, or

potential punishment authorized by the Uniform Code of Military Justice (UCMJ). A unit commander shall not conduct internal command-directed investigations on sexual assault (i.e., no referrals to appointed command investigators or inquiry officers) or delay immediately contacting NCIS or the cognizant MCIO while attempting to assess the credibility of the report.

(2) Commander(s) of the Service member(s) who is a subject of a sexual assault allegation shall immediately provide in writing all disposition data, to include any administrative or judicial action taken, stemming from the sexual assault investigation to the MCIO. Dispositions on cases referred by MCIOs to other DoD law enforcement agencies shall be immediately reported to the MCIOs upon their final disposition. MCIOs shall request dispositions on referred cases from civilian law enforcement agencies and, if received, those dispositions shall be immediately reported by the MCIO in the Defense Sexual Assault Incident Database (DSAID) in order to meet the congressional annual reporting requirements. When requested by MCIOs and other DoD law enforcement, commanders shall provide final disposition of sexual assault cases. Final case disposition is required to be inputted into DSAID.

(3) If the MCIO has been notified of the disposition in a civilian sexual assault case, the MCIO shall notify the commander of this disposition immediately.

i. Appoint a point of contact to serve as a formal liaison between the installation SARC and the installation Family Advocacy Program (FAP) and domestic violence intervention and prevention staff (or civilian domestic resource if FAP is not available for a Reserve Component victim) to direct coordination when a sexual assault occurs within a domestic relationship or involves child abuse.

j. Ensure appropriate training of all military responders be directed and documented in accordance with training standards in enclosure (10) of this Instruction. Direct and document appropriate training of all military responders who attend the CMG.

k. Identify and maintain a liaison with civilian sexual assault victim resources. Where necessary, it is strongly recommended that a Memorandum of Understanding (MOU) or

Memorandum of Agreement (MOA) with the appropriate local authorities and civilian service organizations be established to maximize cooperation, reciprocal reporting of sexual assault information, and consultation regarding jurisdiction for the prosecution of Service members involved in sexual assault, as appropriate.

l. Require that each Service member who reports a sexual assault, pursuant to the respective Military Service regulations, be given the opportunity to consult with legal assistance counsel, and in cases where the victim may have been involved in collateral misconduct, to consult with defense counsel. Victims shall be referred to the Victim Witness Assistance Program (VWAP). Information concerning the prosecution shall be provided to victims in accordance with VWAP procedures. The Service member victim shall be informed of this opportunity to consult with legal assistance counsel as soon as the victim seeks assistance from a SARC, SAPR VA, or any DoD law enforcement agent or judge advocate.

m. Direct that DoD law enforcement agents and VWAP personnel provide victims of sexual assault who elect an Unrestricted Report with appropriate information throughout the investigative and legal process. The completed "Initial Information for Victims and Witnesses of Crime" form (DD Form 2701) shall be distributed to the victim in Unrestricted Reporting cases by DoD law enforcement agents.

n. Protect sexual assault victims from coercion, discrimination, or reprisals. Commanders shall protect SARCs and SAPR VAs from coercion, discrimination, or reprisals related to the execution of their SAPR duties and responsibilities.

o. Require that sexual assault reports be entered into DSAID through interface with a Military Service data system, or by direct data entry by authorized personnel. Only SARCs who have, at a minimum, a favorable National Agency Check (NAC) shall be permitted access to enter sexual assault reports into DSAID.

p. Designate an official, usually the SARC, to generate an alpha-numeric Restricted Reporting Case Number (RRCN).

q. Commanders are encouraged to be responsive to a victim's desire to discuss his or her case with the installation commander tasked by the Military Service with oversight responsibility for the SAPR program.

4. <u>MOUs or MOAs with Local Civilian Authorities</u>. The purpose of MOUs and MOAs is to:

a. Enhance communications and the sharing of information regarding sexual assault prosecutions, as well as of the sexual assault care and forensic examinations that involve Service members and eligible TRICARE beneficiaries covered by this Instruction.

b. Collaborate with local community crisis counseling centers, as necessary, to augment or enhance their sexual assault programs.

c. Provide liaison with private or public sector sexual assault councils, as appropriate.

d. Provide information about medical and counseling services related to care for victims of sexual assault in the civilian community, when not otherwise available at the MTFs, in order that military victims may be offered the appropriate healthcare and civilian resources, where available and where covered by military healthcare benefits.

e. Where appropriate or required by MOU or MOA, facilitate training for civilian service providers about SAPR policy and the roles and responsibilities of the SARC and SAPR VA.

5. <u>Line of Duty (LOD) Procedures</u>

a. Members of the Reserve Components, whether they file a Restricted or Unrestricted Report, shall have access to medical treatment and counseling for injuries and illness incurred from a sexual assault inflicted upon a Service member when performing active duty service and inactive duty training.

b. Medical entitlements remain dependent on a LOD determination as to whether or not the sexual assault incident occurred in an active duty or inactive duty training status. However, regardless of their duty status at the time that the sexual assault incident occurred, or at the time that they are seeking SAPR services (see enclosure (2)), Reserve Component members can elect either the Restricted or Unrestricted Reporting option and have access to the SAPR services of a SARC and a SAPR VA.

c. The following LOD procedures shall be followed by Reserve Component commanders.

(1) LOD determinations may be made without the victim being identified to DoD law enforcement or command, solely for the purpose of enabling the victim to access medical care and psychological counseling, and without identifying injuries from sexual assault as the cause.

(2) When assessing LOD determinations for sexual assault victims, the commander of the Reserve command in each Service shall designate individuals within their respective organizations to process LODs for victims of sexual assault when performing active service and inactive duty training.

(a) Designated individuals shall possess the maturity and experience to assist in a sensitive situation and, if dealing with a Restricted Report, to safeguard confidential communications. These individuals are specifically authorized to receive confidential communications for the purpose of determining LOD status.

(b) The appropriate SARC will brief the designated individuals on Restricted Reporting policies, exceptions to Restricted Reporting, and the limitations of disclosure of confidential communications (see enclosure (4)). The SARC and these individuals may consult with their servicing legal office, in the same manner as other recipients of privileged information for assistance, exercising due care to protect confidential communications by disclosing only non-identifying information. Unauthorized disclosure may result in disciplinary action (see enclosure (4)).

(3) For LOD purposes, the victim's SARC may provide documentation that substantiates the victim's duty status as well as the filing of the Restricted Report to the designated official.

(4) If medical or mental healthcare is required beyond initial treatment and follow-up, a licensed medical or mental health provider must recommend a continued treatment plan.

(5) When evaluating pay and entitlements, the modification of the LOD process for Restricted Reporting does not extend to pay and allowances or travel and transportation incident to the healthcare entitlement. However, at any time the Service member may request an unrestricted LOD to be completed in order to receive the full range of entitlements.

(6) Continuation and return to active duty pending LOD determination for response to sexual assault.

(a) In the case of a member of a Reserve Component who is the alleged victim of sexual assault committed while on active duty and who is expected to be released from active duty before the LOD determination is made, the Chief of Naval Operations (CNO) or the Commandant of the Marine Corps (CMC), upon request of the member, may order the member to be retained on active duty until completion of the LOD determination (see reference (m)). Eligible members shall be informed as soon as practicable after the alleged assault of the option to request continuation on active duty for this purpose.

(b) Return to Active Duty. In the case of a member of a Reserve Component not on active duty who is the alleged victim of a sexual assault that occurred while the member was on active duty and when the LOD determination is not completed, the CNO or CMC, upon request of the member, may order the member to active duty for such time as necessary for completion of the LOD determination (see reference (m)).

(c) A request submitted by a member of a Reserve Component as above to continue on active duty, or to be ordered to active duty, respectively, must be decided within 30 days from the date of the request. If the request is denied, the member may appeal to the first General Officer or Flag Officer in the chain of command of the member, and in the case of such an appeal a decision on the appeal must be made within 15 days from the date of the appeal.

6. <u>Expedited Victim Transfer Requests</u>

    a. Any threat to life or safety of a Service member shall be immediately reported to command and DoD law enforcement authorities (see enclosure (2)) and a request to transfer the victim under these circumstances will be handled in accordance with established Service regulations.

    b. Service members who file an Unrestricted Report of sexual assault shall be informed by the SARC, SAPR VA, or the Service member's Commanding Officer (CO) at the time of making the report, or as soon as practicable, of the option to request a temporary or permanent expedited transfer from their assigned command or installation, or to a different location within their assigned command or installation. The Service members shall initiate the transfer request and submit the request to their COs. The CO shall document the date and time the request is received.

        (1) A presumption shall be established in favor of transferring a Service member (who initiated the transfer request) following a credible report (see enclosure (2)) of sexual assault. The CO, or the appropriate approving authority, shall make a credible report determination at the time the expedited request is made after considering the advice of the supporting judge advocate, or other legal advisor concerned, and the available evidence based on an MCIO's investigation's information (if available).

        (2) Expedited transfers of Service members who report that they are victims of sexual assault shall be limited to sexual assault offenses reported in the form of an Unrestricted Report.

            (a) This Instruction does not address victims covered under the Family Advocacy Program (FAP).

            (b) If the Service member files a Restricted Report and requests an expedited transfer, the Service member must affirmatively change his or her reporting option to Unrestricted Reporting on the DD Form 2910, in order to be eligible for an expedited transfer.

(3) When the alleged perpetrator is the commander or otherwise in the victim's chain of command, the SARC shall inform such victims of the opportunity to go outside the chain of command to report the offense to MCIOs, other commanding officers or an Inspector General (IG). Victims shall be informed that they can also seek assistance from a legal assistance attorney or the DoD Safe Helpline.

(4) The CO shall expeditiously process a transfer request from a command or installation, or to a different location within the command or installation. The CO shall request and take into consideration the Service member's input before making a decision involving a temporary or permanent transfer and the location of the transfer. If approved, the transfer orders shall also include the Service member's dependents or military spouse (as applicable). The CO shall also inform the appropriate MCIO of an impending expedited transfer of a victim.

(5) The CO must approve or disapprove a Service member's request for a Permanent Change of Station (PCS), Permanent Change of Assignment (PCA), or unit transfer within 72 hours from receipt of the Service member's request. The decision to approve the request shall be immediately forwarded to the designated activity (see enclosure (2)) that processes PCS, PCA, or unit transfers.

(6) If the Service member's transfer request is disapproved by the CO, the Service member shall be given the opportunity to request review by the first General or Flag Officer (G/FO) in the chain of command of the member, or an SES equivalent (if applicable). The decision to approve or disapprove the request for transfer must be made within 72 hours of submission of the request for review. If a civilian Senior Executive Service (SES) equivalent reviewer approves the transfer, the Secretary of the Navy (SECNAV) shall process and issue orders for the transfer.

(7) The Services shall make every reasonable effort to minimize disruption to the normal career progression of a Service member who reports that he or she is a victim of a sexual assault.

(8) Expedited transfer procedures require that a CO or the appropriate approving authority make a determination and provide his or her reasons and justification on the transfer of a Service member based on a credible report of sexual assault. A CO shall consider:

(a) The Service member's reasons for the request.

(b) Potential transfer of the alleged offender instead of the Service member requesting the transfer.

(c) Nature and circumstances of the offense.

(d) Whether a temporary transfer would meet the Service member's needs and the operational needs of the unit.

(e) Training status of the Service member requesting the transfer.

(f) Availability of positions within other units on the installation.

(g) Status of the investigation and potential impact on the investigation and future disposition of the offense, after consultation with the investigating MCIOs.

(h) Location of the alleged offender.

(i) Alleged offender's status (Service member or civilian).

(j) Other pertinent circumstances or facts.

(9) Service members requesting the transfer shall be informed that they may have to return for the prosecution of the case, if the determination is made that prosecution is the appropriate command action.

(10) Commanders shall directly counsel the Service member to ensure that he or she is fully informed regarding:

(a) Reasonably foreseeable career impacts.

(b) The potential impact of the transfer or reassignment on the investigation and case disposition or the initiation of other adverse action against the alleged offender.

(c) The effect on bonus recoupment (if, for example, they cannot work in their specialty or Military Occupational Specialty).

(d) Other possible consequences of granting the request.

(11) Require that expedited transfer procedures for Reserve Component members who make Unrestricted Reports of sexual assault be established by commanders within available resources and authorities. If requested by the Service member, the command should allow for separate training on different weekends or times from the alleged offender or with a different unit in the home drilling location to ensure undue burden is not placed on the Service member and his or her family by the transfer. Potential transfer of the alleged offender instead of the Service member should also be considered. At a minimum, the alleged offender's access to the Service member who made the Unrestricted Report shall be controlled, as appropriate.

(12) Even in those court-martial cases in which the accused has been acquitted, the standard for approving an expedited transfer still remains whether a credible report has been filed. The commander shall consider all the facts and circumstances surrounding the case and the basis for the transfer request.

7. <u>Military Protective Orders (MPOs)</u>. In Unrestricted Reporting cases, commanders shall execute the following procedures regarding MPOs:

a. Require the SARC or the SAPR VA to inform sexual assault victims protected by an MPO, in a timely manner, of the option to request transfer from the assigned command.

b. Notify the appropriate civilian authorities of the issuance of an MPO and of the individuals involved in the order, in the event an MPO has been issued against a Service member and any individual involved in the MPO does not reside on a military installation at any time during the duration of the MPO.

(1) An MPO issued by a military commander shall remain in effect until such time as the commander terminates the order or issues a replacement order.

(2) The issuing commander shall notify the appropriate civilian authorities of any change made in an MPO, or its termination.

(3) When an MPO has been issued against a Service member and any individual involved in the MPO does not reside on a military installation at any time during the duration of the MPO, notify the NCIS and appropriate civilian authorities of the issuance of an MPO and of the individuals involved in the order. The appropriate civilian authorities shall include, at a minimum, the local civilian law enforcement agency or agencies with jurisdiction to respond to an emergency call from the residence of any individual involved in the order.

c. Advise the person seeking the MPO that the MPO is not enforceable by civilian authorities off base and that victims desiring protection off base should seek a Civilian Protective Order (CPO). Off base violations of the MPO should be reported to the issuing commander, DoD law enforcement, and the relevant MCIO for investigation.

(1) A CPO shall have the same force and effect on a military installation as such order has within the jurisdiction of the civilian court that issued such order. Commanders, MCIOs, and installation DoD law enforcement personnel shall take all reasonable measures necessary to ensure that a CPO is given full force and effect on all DoD installations within the jurisdiction of the civilian court that issued such order.

(2) If the victim has informed the SARC of an existing CPO, a commander shall require the SARC to inform the CMG of the existence of the CPO and its requirements. After the CPO information is received at the CMG, DoD law enforcement agents shall be required to document CPOs for all Service members in their investigative case file, to include documentation for Reserve Component personnel in title 10 status.

d. Note that MPOs in cases other than sexual assault matters may have separate requirements.

e. Issuing commanders fill out the "Military Protective Order (MPO)" (DD Form 2873) and provide victims and alleged offenders with copies of the completed form. Verbal MPOs can be issued, but need to be subsequently documented with a DD Form 2873, as soon as possible.

f. Require DoD law enforcement agents document MPOs for all Service members in their investigative case file, to include documentation for Reserve Component personnel in title 10 status. The appropriate DoD law enforcement agent representative to the CMG shall brief the CMG chair and co-chair on the existence of an MPO.

g. If the commander's decision is to deny the MPO request, document the reasons for the denial. Denials of MPO requests go to the installation commander or equivalent command level (in consultation with a judge advocate) for the final decision.

8. Collateral Misconduct in Sexual Assault Cases

a. Collateral misconduct by the victim of a sexual assault is one of the most significant barriers to reporting assault because of the victim's fear of punishment. Some reported sexual assaults involve circumstances where the victim may have engaged in some form of misconduct (e.g., underage drinking or other related alcohol offenses, adultery, fraternization, or other violations of certain regulations or orders). Commanders shall have discretion to defer action on alleged collateral misconduct by the sexual assault victims (and shall not be penalized for such a deferral decision), until final disposition of the sexual assault case, taking into account the trauma to the victim and responding appropriately so as to encourage reporting of sexual assault and continued victim cooperation, while also bearing in mind any potential speedy trial and statute of limitations concerns.

b. The initial disposition authority is withheld from all commanders within the DON who do not possess at least special court-martial convening authority and who are not in the grade of 0-6 (i.e., Colonel or Navy Captain) or higher, with respect to the alleged offenses of rape, sexual assault, forcible sodomy, and all attempts to commit such offenses, in violation of Articles 120, 125, and 80 of the Uniform Code of Military Justice (UCMJ). Commanders may defer taking action on a victim's alleged collateral misconduct arising from or that relates to the sexual assault incident until the initial disposition action for the sexual assault investigation is completed.

c. Commanders and supervisors should take appropriate action for the victim's alleged collateral misconduct (if warranted), responding appropriately in order to encourage sexual assault reporting and continued cooperation, while avoiding those actions that may further traumatize the victim. Ultimately, victim cooperation should significantly enhance timely and effective investigations, as well as the appropriate disposition of sexual assaults.

d. Subordinate commanders shall be advised that taking action on a victim's alleged collateral misconduct may be deferred until final disposition of the sexual assault case. Commanders and supervisors shall not be penalized for deferring alleged collateral misconduct actions for the sexual assault victim until final disposition of the sexual assault case.

e. Commanders shall have the authority to determine, in a timely manner, how to best manage the disposition of alleged misconduct, to include making the decision to defer disciplinary actions regarding a victim's alleged collateral misconduct until after the final disposition of the sexual assault case, where appropriate. For those sexual assault cases for which the victim's alleged collateral misconduct is deferred, Military Service reporting and processing requirements should take such deferrals into consideration and allow for the time deferred to be subtracted, when evaluating whether a commander took too long to resolve the collateral misconduct.

9. <u>Commander SAPR Prevention Procedures</u>. Each commander shall implement a SAPR prevention program that:

a. Establishes a command climate of sexual assault prevention predicated on mutual respect and trust, recognizes and embraces diversity, and values the contributions of all its Service members.

b. Emphasizes that sexual assault is a crime and violates the Core Values of being a professional in the Military Services and ultimately destroys unit cohesion and the trust that is essential for mission readiness and success.

c.   Emphasizes DoD and Military Service policies on sexual assault and the potential legal consequences for those who commit such crimes.

d.   Monitors the organization's SAPR climate and responds with appropriate action toward any negative trends that may emerge.

e.   Identifies and remedies environmental factors specific to the location that may facilitate the commission of sexual assaults (e.g., insufficient lighting).

f.   Emphasizes sexual assault prevention training for all assigned personnel.

g.   Establishes prevention training that focuses on the continuum of harm and identifying the behavior of potential offenders.

SEXUAL ASSAULT RESPONSE COORDINATOR AND
SEXUAL ASSAULT PREVENTION AND RESPONSE VICTIM ADVOCATE
PROCEDURES

1. <u>Sexual Assault Response Coordinator (SARC) Procedures</u>. The SARC shall:

    a. Serve as the single point of contact to coordinate sexual assault response when a sexual assault is reported. All SARCs shall be authorized to perform victim advocate duties in accordance with Military Service regulations.

    b. In accordance with the Department of Defense (DoD) Sexual Assault Advocate Certification Program (D-SAACP), comply with DoD Sexual Assault Advocate Certification requirements.

    c. Be trained in and understand the confidentiality requirements of Restricted Reporting and of Military Rule of Evidence (MRE) 514. Training must include exceptions to Restricted Reporting and MRE 514.

    d. Assist the installation commander in ensuring that victims of sexual assault receive appropriate responsive care and understand their available reporting options (Restricted and Unrestricted) and available Sexual Assault Prevention and Response (SAPR) services.

    e. Be authorized by this Instruction to accept reports of sexual assault along with the Sexual Assault Prevention and Response Victim Advocate (SAPR VA) and healthcare personnel.

    f. Report directly to the installation commander in accordance with reference (b), to include providing regular updates to the installation commander and assist the commander to meet annual SAPR training requirements, including providing orientation briefings for newly assigned personnel and, as appropriate, providing community education publicizing available SAPR services.

    g. Provide a 24-hour, 7-days-per-week response capability to victims of sexual assault, to include deployed areas.

        (1) SARCs shall respond to every Restricted and Unrestricted Report of sexual assault on a military installation

and the response shall be in person, unless otherwise requested by the victim.

(2) Based on the locality, the SARC may ask the SAPR VA to respond and speak to the victim.

(a) There will be situations where a sexual assault victim receives medical care and a Sexual Assault Forensic Exam (SAFE) outside of a military installation under a Memorandum of Understanding (MOU) or Memorandum of Agreement (MOA) with local private or public sector entities. In these cases, pursuant to the MOU or MOA, victims shall be asked whether they would like the SARC to be notified, and, if so, the SARC or SAPR VA shall be notified, and a SARC or SAPR VA shall respond.

(b) When contacted by the SARC or SAPR VA, a sexual assault victim can elect not to speak to the SARC or SAPR VA, or the sexual assault victim may ask to schedule an appointment at a later time to speak to the SARC or SAPR VA.

(3) SARCs shall provide a response that recognizes the high prevalence of pre-existing trauma (prior to the present sexual assault incident).

(4) SARCs shall provide a response that is gender-responsive, culturally-competent, and recovery-oriented.

(5) SARCs shall offer appropriate referrals to sexual assault victims and facilitate access to referrals. Provide referrals at the request of the victim.

(a) Encourage sexual assault victims to follow-up with the referrals and facilitate these referrals, as appropriate.

(b) In order to competently facilitate referrals, inquire whether the victim is a Reservist or a National Guard (NG) member to ensure that victims are referred to the appropriate geographic location.

h. Explain to the victim that the services of the SARC and SAPR VA are optional and these services may be declined, in whole or in part, at any time. The victim may decline advocacy services, even if the SARC or SAPR VA holds a position of higher rank or authority than the victim. Explain to victims the option of requesting a different SAPR VA (subject to availability, depending on locality staffing) or continuing without SAPR VA services.

   (1) Explain the available reporting options to the victim.

      (a) Have the victim fill out the "Victim Reporting Preference Statement" (DD Form 2910) where the victim elects to make a Restricted or Unrestricted Report.

      (b) Inform the victim that the DD Form 2910 will be uploaded to Defense Sexual Assault Incident Database (DSAID) and maintained for 50 years in Unrestricted Reports and retained in hard copy for 5 years in Restricted Reports, for the purpose of providing the victim access to document their sexual assault victimization with the Veterans Administration (VA) for care and benefits. However, at the request of a Service member who files a Restricted Report on an incident of sexual assault, the DD Form 2910 and the "DoD Sexual Assault Forensic Examination (SAFE) Report" (DD Form 2911) filed in connection with the Restricted Report shall be retained for 50 years.

      (c) The SARC or SAPR VA shall tell the victim of any local or State sexual assault reporting requirements that may limit the possibility of Restricted Reporting. At the same time, the victims shall be briefed of the protections and exceptions to Military Rule of Evidence (MRE) 514.

   (2) Give the victim a hard copy of the DD Form 2910 with the victim's signature.

      (a) Advise the victim to keep the copy of the DD Form 2910 in their personal permanent records as this form may be used by the victim in other matters before other agencies (e.g., Department of Veterans Affairs) or for any other lawful purpose.

      (b) Store the original DD Form 2910 pursuant to secure storage Military Service regulations and privacy laws. A SARC being reassigned shall be required to assure their supervisor of the secure transfer of stored DD Forms 2910 to the next SARC. In the event of transitioning SARCs, the departing

SARC shall inform their supervisor of the secure storage location of the DD Forms 2910, and the SARC supervisor will ensure the safe transfer of the DD Forms 2910.

(3) Explain SAFE confidentiality to victims and the confidentiality of the contents of the SAFE Kit.

(4) Explain the implications of a victim confiding in another person resulting in a third-party report to command or DoD law enforcement (see enclosure (4) of this Instruction).

(5) Provide the installation commander with information regarding an Unrestricted Report within 24 hours of an Unrestricted Report of sexual assault. This notification may be extended to 48 hours after the Unrestricted Report of the incident if there are extenuating circumstances in the deployed environments.

(6) Provide the installation commander with non-Personally Identifiable Information (non-PII) within 24 hours of a Restricted Report of sexual assault. This notification may be extended to 48 hours after the Restricted Report of the incident if there are extenuating circumstances in a deployed environment. Command and installation demographics shall be taken into account when determining the information to be provided.

(7) Exercise oversight responsibility for SAPR VAs authorized to respond to sexual assaults when they are providing victim advocacy services.

(8) Perform victim advocacy duties, as needed. DoD recognizes the SARC's authority to perform duties as SAPR VAs, even though the SARC may not be designated in writing as a SAPR VA pursuant to Military Service regulation.

(9) Inform the victim of the opportunity to consult with legal assistance counsel, and in cases where the victim may have been involved in collateral misconduct, to consult with defense counsel.

(a) Inform the victim that information concerning the prosecution shall be provided to them in accordance with references (g) and (h).

(b) The Service member victim shall be informed of the opportunity to consult with legal assistance counsel as soon as the victim seeks assistance from a SARC or SAPR VA.

(10) Facilitate education of command personnel on sexual assault and victim advocacy services.

(11) Facilitate briefings on victim advocacy services to Service members, military dependents, DoD civilian employees outside the continental United States (OCONUS), DoD contractors (accompanying the Military Services in contingency operations OCONUS), and other command or installation personnel, as appropriate.

(12) Facilitate annual SAPR training.

(13) Facilitate the development and collaboration of SAPR public awareness campaigns for victims of sexual assault, including planning local events for Sexual Assault Awareness and Prevention Month. Publicize the DoD Safe Helpline on all outreach materials.

(14) Coordinate medical and counseling services between military installations and deployed units related to care for victims of sexual assault.

(15) Conduct an ongoing assessment of the consistency and effectiveness of the SAPR program within the assigned area of responsibility.

(16) Collaborate with other agencies and activities to improve SAPR responses to and support of victims of sexual assault.

(17) Maintain liaison with commanders, DoD law enforcement, Naval Criminal Investigative Service (NCIS) and other Military Criminal Investigative Organizations (MCIOs), and civilian authorities, as appropriate, for the purpose of facilitating the following protocols and procedures to:

(a) Activate victim advocacy 24 hours a day, 7 days a week for all incidents of reported sexual assault occurring either on or off the installation involving Service members and other persons covered by this Instruction.

(b) Collaborate on public safety, awareness, and prevention measures.

(c) Facilitate ongoing training of DoD and civilian law enforcement and criminal investigative personnel on the SAPR policy and program and the roles and responsibilities of the SARC and SAPR VAs.

(18) Consult with command legal representatives, healthcare personnel, and MCIOs, (or when feasible, civilian law enforcement), to assess the potential impact of State laws governing the reporting requirements for adult sexual assault that may affect compliance with the Restricted Reporting option and develop or revise applicable MOUs and MOAs, as appropriate.

(19) Collaborate with MTFs within their respective areas of responsibility to establish protocols and procedures to direct notification of the SARC and SAPR VA for all incidents of reported sexual assault, and facilitate ongoing training of healthcare personnel on the roles and responsibilities of the SARC and SAPR VAs.

(20) Collaborate with local private or public sector entities that provide medical care to Service members or TRICARE eligible beneficiaries who care for sexual assault victims and offer a SAFE outside of a military installation through an MOU or MOA.

(a) Establish protocols and procedures with these local private or public sector entities to facilitate direct notification of the SARC for all incidents of reported sexual assault and facilitate training of healthcare personnel of local private or public sector entities on the roles and responsibilities of SARCs and SAPR VAs, for Service members and persons covered by this policy.

(b) Provide off installation referrals to the sexual assault victims, as needed.

(21) When a victim has a temporary or permanent change of station or is deployed, immediately request victim consent in writing to transfer case management documents, which shall be documented on the DD Form 2910. Upon receipt of victim consent, expeditiously transfer case management documents to ensure

continuity of care and SAPR services. If the SARC has already closed the case and terminated victim contact, no other action is needed. However, when the SARC has a temporary change of station or permanent change of station or is deployed, no victim consent is required to transfer the case to the next SARC. Every effort must be made to inform the victim of the case transfer. In the SARC has already closed the case and terminated victim contact, no other action is needed.

(22) Document and track the services referred to and requested by the victim from the time of the initial report of a sexual assault through the final case disposition or until the victim no longer desires services.

(a) Enter information into DSAID either through direct data entry by SARCs or by Military Service DSAID interface within 48 hours of the report of sexual assault. In deployed locations that have internet connectivity issues, the time frame is extended to 96 hours. Only SARCs who have, at a minimum, a favorable National Agency Check (NAC) shall be permitted access to enter sexual assault reports into DSAID.

(b) Maintain in DSAID, or the DSAID-interfaced Military Service data system, an account of the services referred to and requested by the victim for all reported sexual assault incidents, from medical treatment through counseling, and from the time of the initial report of a sexual assault through the final case disposition or until the victim no longer desires services.

(23) Provide information to assist installation commanders to manage trends and characteristics of sexual assault crimes at the Military Service-level and mitigate the risk factors that may be present within the associated environment (e.g., the necessity for better lighting in the showers or latrines and in the surrounding area).

(24) Participate in the Case Management Group (CMG) to review individual cases of Unrestricted Reports of sexual assault.

(a) The installation SARC shall serve as the co-chair of the CMG. This responsibility is not delegable. If an installation has multiple SARCs on the installation, a Lead SARC shall be designated by the Service concerned, and shall serve as the co-chair.

(b) Other SARCs and SAPR VAs shall actively participate in each CMG meeting by presenting oral updates on their assigned sexual assault victim cases, providing recommendations and, if needed, seeking assistance from the chair or victim's commander.

(25) Familiarize the unit commanders and supervisors of SAPR VAs with the SAPR VA roles and responsibilities, using the "Victim Advocate Supervisor Statement of Understanding" (DD Form 2909).

2. SAPR VA Procedures

a. The SAPR VA shall:

(1) In accordance with the D-SAACP, comply with DoD Sexual Assault Advocate Certification requirements.

(2) Be trained in and understand the confidentiality requirements of Restricted Reporting and MRE 514. Training must include exceptions to Restricted Reporting and MRE 514.

(3) Facilitate care and provide referrals and non-clinical support to the adult victim of a sexual assault.

(a) Support will include providing information on available options and resources so the victim can make informed decisions about his or her case.

(b) The SAPR VA will be directly accountable to the SARC in adult sexual assault cases (not under the Family Advocacy Program (FAP) jurisdiction) and shall provide victim advocacy for adult victims of sexual assault.

(4) Acknowledge their understanding of their advocacy roles and responsibilities using DD Form 2909.

b. At the Military Service's discretion, victim advocacy may be provided by a Service member or DoD civilian employee. Personnel responsible for providing victim advocacy shall:

(1) Be notified and immediately respond upon receipt of a report of sexual assault.

(2) Provide coordination and encourage victim service referrals and ongoing, non-clinical support to the victim of a reported sexual assault and facilitate care in accordance with the Sexual Assault Response Protocols prescribed SAPR Policy Toolkit located on www.sapr.mil. Assist the victim in navigating those processes required to obtain care and services needed. It is neither the SAPR VA's role nor responsibility to be the victim's mental health provider or to act as an investigator.

(3) Report directly to the SARC while carrying out sexual assault advocacy responsibilities.

HEALTHCARE PROVIDER PROCEDURES

1. This enclosure provides guidance on the medical management of victims of sexual assault to ensure standardized, timely, accessible, and comprehensive healthcare for victims of sexual assault, to include the ability to elect a Sexual Assault Forensic Exam (SAFE) Kit. This policy is applicable to all Department of Navy (DON) healthcare personnel who provide or coordinate medical care for victims of sexual assault covered by this Instruction.

2. Sexual assault victims shall be given priority, and treated as emergency cases. Emergency care shall consist of emergency medical care and the offer of a SAFE. Even when they decline a SAFE Kit, victims shall be advised of available services and encouraged (but not mandated) to receive medical care, psychological care, and victim advocacy.

    a. Standardized Medical Care. To ensure standardized healthcare, the Chief, Bureau of Medicine and Surgery (CHBUMED) shall:

        (1) Establish minimum standards of medical treatment for victims of sexual assault based on requirements outlined in the Department of Justice National Protocol (reference (d)).

        (2) When drafting Memoranda of Understanding (MOUs) or Memoranda of Agreement (MOAs) with local civilian medical facilities to provide DoD-reimbursable healthcare (to include psychological care) and forensic examinations for Service members and TRICARE eligible sexual assault victims, the following provisions shall be required:

            (a) Ask the victim whether he or she would like the SARC to be notified, and if yes, a SARC or SAPR VA shall respond.

            (b) Local private or public sector providers shall have processes and procedures in place to assess that local community standards meet or exceed those set forth in reference (d) as a condition of the MOUs or MOAs. Medical Treatment Facilities (MTFs) shall verify initially and periodically that the civilian entities meet or exceed standards for conducting forensic exams of adult sexual assault victims outlined in reference (d).

(3) Ensure that DON healthcare providers providing care to sexual assault victims in remote areas or while deployed have access to the current version of reference (d) for conducting forensic exams.

(4) Implement procedures to provide the victim information regarding the availability of a SAFE Kit, which the victim has the option of refusing. If performed in the MTF, the healthcare provider shall use a DoD SAFE Kit and the current edition of the "DoD Sexual Assault Forensic Examination (SAFE) Report" form (DD Form 2911).

(5) Ensure that SARCs are notified of all incidents of sexual assault in accordance with reporting procedures outlined in enclosure (4).

(a) Ensure that processes are established to support coordination between healthcare personnel and the SARC.

(b) If a victim initially seeks assistance at a medical facility, SARC notification must not delay the emergency treatment of a victim.

(6) Require that care provided to sexual assault victims is gender-responsive, culturally competent, and recovery-oriented. Healthcare providers caring for sexual assault victims shall recognize the high prevalence of pre-existing trauma (prior to present sexual assault incident) and the concept of trauma-informed care.

(7) If the healthcare provider is not appropriately trained to collect and preserve a SAFE Kit, require that he or she arrange for a properly trained DoD healthcare provider to do so, if available.

(a) In the absence of a properly trained DoD healthcare provider, the victim shall be offered the option to be transported to a non-DoD healthcare provider for the SAFE Kit, if the victim wants a forensic exam. Victims who are not beneficiaries of the Military Healthcare System shall be advised that they can obtain a SAFE Kit through a local civilian healthcare provider.

(b) When a SAFE Kit is performed at local civilian medical facilities, those facilities are bound by State and local laws, which may require reporting the sexual assault to civilian law enforcement.

(c) If the victim requests to file a report of sexual assault, healthcare personnel shall immediately call a SARC or Sexual Assault Victim Advocate (SAPR VA), to assure the victim is offered Sexual Assault Prevention and Response (SAPR) services and so that a "Victim Reporting Preference Statement" (DD Form 2910) can be completed.

(8) Ensure that SAFE Kit evidence collection procedures are the same for a Restricted and an Unrestricted Report of sexual assault.

(a) Upon completion of the SAFE Kit and securing of the evidence, the healthcare provider will turn over the material to Naval Criminal Investigative Service (NCIS) or NCIS Consolidated Evidence Facility representative or the appropriate Military Service-designated law enforcement agency or Military Criminal Investigative Organization (MCIO) as determined by the selected reporting option.

(b) Upon completion of the SAFE Kit, the sexual assault victim shall be provided with a hard copy of the completed DD Form 2911. Advise the victim to keep the copy of the DD Form 2911 in their personal permanent records as this form may be used by the victim in other matters before other agencies (e.g., Department of Veterans Affairs) or for any other lawful purpose.

(9) Publicize availability of medical treatment (to include behavioral health), and referral services for alleged offenders who are also active duty Service members.

(10) Establish procedures for the healthcare provider, in the course of preparing a SAFE Kit for Restricted Reports of sexual assault:

(a) Contact the SARC, who shall generate an alpha-numeric Restricted Reporting Case Number (RRCN) unique to each incident. The RRCN shall be used in lieu of Personally Identifiable Information (PII) to label and identify evidence

collected from a SAFE Kit (e.g., accompanying documentation, personal effects, and clothing). The SARC shall provide (or the SARC will designate the SAPR VA to provide) the healthcare provider with the RRCN to use in place of PII.

(b) Upon completion of the SAFE Kit, package, seal, and completely label the evidence container(s) with the RRCN and notify NCIS Consolidated Evidence Facility representative or other appropriate Military Service-designated law enforcement agency or MCIO.

(11) Ensure that healthcare personnel maintain the confidentiality of a Restricted Report to include communications with the victim, the SAFE, and the contents of the SAFE Kit, unless an exception to Restricted Reporting applies. Healthcare personnel who make an unauthorized disclosure of a confidential communication are subject to disciplinary action and that unauthorized disclosure has no impact on the status of the Restricted Report; all Restricted Reporting information remains confidential and protected. Improper disclosure of confidential communications under Restricted Reporting, improper release of medical information, and other violations of this guidance are prohibited and may result in discipline pursuant to the UCMJ or State statute, loss of privileges, or other adverse personnel or administrative actions.

b. <u>Timely Medical Care</u>. To comply with the requirement to provide timely medical care, the CHBUMED shall:

(1) Implement processes or procedures giving victims of sexual assault priority as emergency cases.

(2) Provide sexual assault victims with priority treatment as emergency cases, regardless of evidence of physical injury, recognizing that every minute a patient spends waiting to be examined may cause loss of evidence and undue trauma. Priority treatment as emergency cases includes activities relating to access to healthcare, coding, and medical transfer or evacuation, and complete physical assessment, examination,

and treatment of injuries, including immediate emergency interventions.

c. <u>Comprehensive Medical Care</u>. To comply with the requirement to provide comprehensive medical care, the CHBUMED shall:

(1) Establish processes and procedures to coordinate timely access to emergency, follow-up, and specialty care that may be provided in the direct or civilian purchased care sectors for eligible beneficiaries of the Military Health System.

(2) Evaluate and implement, to the extent feasible, processes linking the medical management of the sexually assaulted patient to the primary care manager.

d. <u>Clinically Stable</u>. Require the healthcare provider to consult with the victim, once clinically stable, regarding further healthcare options to the extent eligible, which shall include, but are not limited to:

(1) Testing, prophylactic treatment options, and follow-up care for possible exposure to Human Immunodeficiency Virus (HIV) and other sexually transmitted diseases or infections.

(2) Assessment of the risk of pregnancy, options for emergency contraception, and any necessary follow-up care and referral services.

(3) Assessment of the need for behavioral health services and provisions for a referral, if necessary or requested by the victim.

SEXUAL ASSAULT FORENSIC EXAM
KIT COLLECTION AND PRESERVATION

For the purposes of the Sexual Assault Prevention and Response
(SAPR) Program, forensic evidence collection, and document and
evidence retention shall be completed in accordance with this
enclosure pursuant to reference (b), taking into account the
medical condition, needs, requests, and desires of each sexual
assault victim covered by this Instruction.

   a. Medical services offered to eligible victims of sexual
assault include the ability to elect a Sexual Assault Forensic
Exam (SAFE) Kit in addition to the general medical management
related to sexual assault response, to include mental
healthcare. The SAFE of a sexual assault victim should be
conducted by a healthcare provider who has specialized education
and clinical experience in the collection of forensic evidence
and treatment of these victims. The forensic component includes
gathering information in the "DoD Sexual Assault Forensic
Examination (SAFE) Report" (DD Form 2911) from the victim for
the medical forensic history, an examination, documentation of
biological and physical findings, collection of evidence from
the victim, and follow-up as needed to document additional
evidence.

   b. The process for collecting and preserving sexual assault
evidence for the Restricted Reporting option is the same as the
Unrestricted Reporting option, except that the Restricted
Reporting option does not trigger the official investigative
process, and any evidence collected has to be placed inside the
SAFE Kit, which is marked with the Restricted Reporting Case
Number (RRCN) in the location where the victim's name would have
otherwise been written. The victim's SAFE and accompanying Kit
is treated as a confidential communication under this reporting
option. The healthcare provider shall encourage the victim to
obtain referrals for additional medical, psychological,
chaplain, victim advocacy, or other SAPR services, as needed.
The victim shall be informed that the Sexual Assault Response
Coordinator (SARC) will assist them in accessing SAPR services.

   c. In situations where installations do not have a SAFE
capability, the installation commander will require that the
eligible victim, who wishes to have a SAFE, be transported to a
Medical Treatment Facility (MTF) or local off-base, non-military

facility that has a SAFE capability. A local sexual assault nurse examiner or other healthcare providers who are trained and credentialed to perform a SAFE may also be contracted to report to the MTF to conduct the examination.

d. The Sexual Assault Response Coordinator (SARC) or Sexual Assault Prevention and Response Victim Advocate (SAPR VA) shall tell the victim of any local or State sexual assault reporting requirements that may limit the possibility of Restricted Reporting before proceeding with the SAFE.

e. Upon completion of the SAFE in an Unrestricted Reporting case, the healthcare provider shall package, seal, and label the evidence container(s) with the victim's name and notify the Naval Criminal Investigative Service (NCIS) or other designated law enforcement agency.

(1) The NCIS representative shall be trained and capable of collecting and preserving evidence to assume custody of the evidence using established chain of custody procedures, consistent with the guidelines published under the authority and oversight of the Department of Defense (DoD) Inspector General (DoDIG).

(2) Memoranda of Understanding (MOUs) and Memoranda of Agreement (MOAs) with off-base, non-military facilities for the purposes of providing medical care to eligible victims of sexual assault covered under this Instruction, shall include instructions for the notification of a SARC (regardless of whether a Restricted or Unrestricted Report of sexual assault is involved), and procedures for the receipt of evidence and disposition of evidence back to NCIS, NCIS Consolidated Evidence Facility representative or other law enforcement agency.

f. Upon completion of the SAFE Kit in a Restricted Reporting case, the healthcare provider shall package, seal, and label the evidence container(s) with the RRCN and store in accordance with Service regulations.

(1) The NCIS Consolidated Evidence Facility representative shall be trained and capable of collecting and preserving evidence to assume custody of the evidence using established chain of custody procedures, consistent with the guidelines published under the authority and oversight of the

DoDIG. MOUs and MOAs, with off-base, non-military facilities for the purpose of providing medical care to eligible victims of sexual assault covered under this Instruction, shall include instructions for the notification of a SARC (regardless of whether a Restricted or Unrestricted Report of sexual assault is involved), procedures for the receipt of evidence, how to request an RRCN, instructions on where to write the RRCN on the SAFE Kit, and disposition of evidence back to NCIS or the NCIS Consolidated Evidence Facility.

(2) Any evidence and the SAFE Kit in Restricted Reporting cases (to include the DD Form 2911) shall be stored for 5 years from the date of the victim's Restricted Report of the sexual assault, thus allowing victims additional time to accommodate, for example, multiple deployments or deployments exceeding 12 months.

(a) The SARC will contact the victim at the 1-year mark of the report to inquire whether the victim wishes to change their reporting option to Unrestricted.

<u>1</u>. If the victim does not change to Unrestricted Reporting, the SARC will explain to the victim that the SAFE Kit, DD Form 2911, and the "Victim Reporting Preference Statement" (DD Form 2910) will be retained for a total of 5 years from the time the victim signed the DD Form 2910 (electing the Restricted Report) and will then be destroyed. The SARC will emphasize to the victim that his or her privacy will be respected and he or she will not be contacted again by the SARC. The SARC will stress it is the victim's responsibility from that point forward, if the victim wishes to change from a Restricted to an Unrestricted Report, to affirmatively contact a SARC before the 5-year retention period elapses. However, at the request of a Service member who files a Restricted Report on an incident of sexual assault, the DD Forms 2910 and 2911 filed in connection with the Restricted Report shall be retained for 50 years.

<u>2</u>. The victim will be advised again to keep a copy of the DD Form 2910 and the DD Form 2911 in his or her personal permanent records as these forms may be used by the victim in other matters with other agencies (e.g., Department of Veterans Affairs) or for any other lawful purpose.

<u>3</u>. If the victim needs another copy of either of these forms, he or she can request it at this point and the SARC shall assist the victim in accessing the requested copies within 7 business days. The SARC will document this request on the DD Form 2910.

(b) At least 30 days before the expiration of the 5-year storage period, NCIS Consolidated Evidence Facility representative shall notify the installation SARC that the storage period is about to expire and confirm with the SARC that the victim has not made a request to change to Unrestricted Reporting or made a request for any personal effects.

<u>1</u>. If there has been no change, then at the expiration of the storage period in compliance with established procedures for the destruction of evidence, NCIS Consolidated Evidence Facility may destroy the evidence maintained under that victim's RRCN.

<u>2</u>. If, before the expiration of the 5-year storage period, a victim changes his or her reporting preference to the Unrestricted Reporting option, the SARC shall notify NCIS, which shall then assume custody of the evidence maintained by the RRCN from NCIS Consolidated Evidence Facility or applicable Service law enforcement agency, according to established chain of custody procedures. NCIS procedures for documenting, maintaining, and storing the evidence shall thereafter be followed.

<u>a</u>. NCIS will receive forensic evidence from the healthcare provider if not already in custody, and label and store such evidence in accordance with established procedures.

<u>b</u>. The designated DoD law enforcement agency or MCIO representative must be trained and capable of collecting and preserving evidence in Restricted Reports prior to assuming custody of the evidence using established chain of custody procedures.

(c) Evidence will be stored by NCIS Consolidated Evidence Facility until the 5-year storage period for Restricted Reporting is reached or a victim changes to Unrestricted Reporting.

CASE MANAGEMENT FOR UNRESTRICTED REPORTS OF SEXUAL ASSAULT

1. General

a. The installation commander or the deputy installation commander shall chair the Case Management Group (CMG) on a monthly basis to review individual cases, facilitate monthly victim updates, and direct system coordination, accountability, entry of disposition and victim access to quality services. This responsibility may not be delegated. If there are no cases in a given month, the CMG will still meet to ensure training, processes, and procedures are complete for the system coordination.

b. The installation Sexual Assault Response Coordinator (SARC) shall serve as the co-chair of the CMG. In the case of multiple SARCs on an installation, then the Lead SARC shall serve this function. This responsibility may not be delegated. Only a SARC who is a Service member or DoD civilian employee may co-chair the multi-disciplinary CMG.

c. Required CMG members shall include: victim's commander; all SARCs assigned to the installation (mandatory attendance regardless of whether they have an assigned victim being discussed); victims' Sexual Assault Prevention and Response Victim Advocate (SAPR VA), Naval Criminal Investigative Service (NCIS) and other DoD law enforcement personnel who are involved with and working on a specific case; victims' healthcare provider or mental health and counseling services provider; chaplain, legal representative, or Staff Judge Advocate (SJA); installation personnel trained to do a safety assessment of current sexual assault victims; victim's Victim Witness Assistance Program (VWAP) representative (or civilian victim witness liaison, if available). NCIS, DoD law enforcement, and the legal representative or SJA shall provide case disposition updates. The CMG chair will ensure that the appropriate principal is available.

d. If the installation is a joint base or if the installation has tenant commands, the commander of the tenant organization and the designated Lead SARC shall be invited to the CMG meetings. The commander of the tenant organization shall provide appropriate information to the host commander, to enable the host commander to provide the necessary supporting services.

e. CMG members shall receive the mandatory SAPR training pursuant to enclosure (10) of this Instruction.

f. Equivalent standards shall be met for case oversight by CMGs in situations where SARCs are not installation-based but instead work within operational and/or deployable organizations.

2. <u>Procedures</u>

a. The CMG members shall carefully consider and implement immediate, short-term, and long-term measures to help facilitate and assure the victim's well-being and recovery from the sexual assault. They will closely monitor the victim's progress and recovery and strive to protect the victim's privacy, ensuring only those with an official need to know have the victim's name and related details. Consequently, where possible, each case shall be reviewed independently bringing in only those personnel associated with the case, as well as the CMG chair and co-chair.

b. The CMG chair shall:

(1) Ensure that commander(s) of the Service member(s), who is a subject of a sexual assault allegation, provide in writing all disposition data, to include any administrative or judicial action taken, stemming from the sexual assault investigation, to NCIS or other appropriate Military Criminal Investigative Organization (MCIO). Information provided by commanders is used to meet the Department's requirements for the submission of criminal history data to the Criminal Justice Information System, Federal Bureau of Investigation; and to record the disposition of offenders into the Defense Sexual Assault Incident Database (DSAID).

(2) Require that case dispositions are communicated to the sexual assault victim within two business days of the final disposition decision. The CMG chair will require that the appropriate paperwork (pursuant to Service regulation) is submitted for each case disposition within 24 hours, which shall be inputted into DSAID or a DSAID Service interface system by the designated officials.

(3) Monitor and require immediate transfer of sexual assault victim information between SARCs and SAPR VAs, in the event of the SARC's or SAPR VA's change of duty station, to ensure continuity of SAPR services for victims.

(4) Require that the SARCs and SAPR VAs actively participate in each CMG meeting by presenting oral updates (without disclosing protected communications and victim confidentiality), providing recommendations and, if needed, the SARC or the SAPR VA shall affirmatively seek assistance from the chair or victim's commander.

(5) Require an update of the status of each expedited transfer request and Military Protective Order (MPO).

(6) If the victim has informed the SARC or SAPR VA of an existing Civilian Protective Order (CPO), the chair shall require the SARC or SAPR VA to inform the CMG of the existence of the CPO and its requirements.

(7) After protective order documentation is presented at the CMG from the SARC or the SAPR VA, the DoD law enforcement agents at the CMG will document the information provided in their investigative case file, to include documentation for Reserve Component personnel in Title 10 status.

c. The CMG Co-chair shall:

(1) Confirm that all reported sexual assaults are entered into DSAID or a DSAID Service interface system within 48 hours of the report of sexual assault. In deployed locations that have internet connectivity issues, the time frame is extended to 96 hours.

(2) Confirm that only the SARC is inputting information into DSAID or a DSAID Service interface system.

(3) Keep minutes of the monthly meetings to include a record of those in attendance and issues discussed. CMG participants are only authorized to share case information with those who have an official need to know.

d. For each victim, the assigned SARC and SAPR VA will confirm at the CMG that the victim has been informed of their

SAPR services to include counseling, medical, and legal resources without violating victim confidentiality.

e. For each victim, each CMG member who is involved with and working on a specific case will provide an oral update without violating victim confidentiality or disclosing privileged communications.

f. For each victim, the victim's commander will confirm at the CMG that the victim has received a monthly update from the victim's commander of her/his case within 72 hours of the last CMG, to assure timely victim updates. This responsibility may not be delegated.

g. On a joint base or if the installation has tenant commands:

(1) The CMG membership will explore the feasibility of joint use of existing SAPR resources, to include rotating on-call status of SARCs and SAPR VAs. Evaluate the effectiveness of communication among SARCs, SAPR VAs, and first responders.

(2) The CMG chair will request an analysis of data to determine trends and patterns of sexual assaults and share this information with the commanders on the joint base or the tenant commands. The CMG membership will be briefed on that trend data.

h. There will be a safety assessment capability. The CMG chair will identify installation personnel who have been trained and are able to perform a safety assessment of each sexual assault victim.

(1) The CMG chair will require designated installation personnel, who have been trained and are able to perform a safety assessment of each sexual assault victim, to become part of the CMG and attend every monthly meeting.

(2) The CMG chair will request a safety assessment by trained personnel of each sexual assault victim at each CMG meeting, to include a discussion of expedited military transfers or MPOs, if needed.

(3) The CMG co-chair will confirm that the victims are advised that MPOs are not enforceable off-base by civilian law enforcement, but any violation should be immediately reported to the command and NCIS for appropriate investigation.

(4) If applicable, the CMG chair will confirm that both the suspect and the victim have a hard copy of the MPO.

(5) Form a High-Risk Response Team if a victim is assessed to be in a high-risk situation. The CMG chair will immediately stand up a multi-disciplinary High-Risk Response Team to continually monitor the victim's safety, by assessing danger and developing a plan to manage the situation.

(a) The High-Risk Response Team shall be chaired by the victim's commander and, at a minimum, include the suspect's commander; the victim's SARC and SAPR VA; the MCIO, the judge advocate, and the VWAP assigned to the case, victim's healthcare provider or mental health and counseling services provider; and the personnel who conducted the safety assessment.

(b) The High-Risk Response Team shall make their first report to the installation commander, CMG chair, and CMG co-chair within 24 hours of being activated. A briefing schedule for the CMG chair and co-chair will be determined, but briefings shall occur at least once a week while the victim is on high-risk status. However, nothing in this section prevents a victim's or suspect's Commanding Officer from taking immediate action to protect and provide care for a victim or restrict access of a suspect to the victim. The commander(s) of both the victim and suspect have the responsibility to ensure the safety and good order and discipline of their members.

(c) The High-Risk Response Team assessment of the victim shall include, but is not limited to evaluating:

1. Victim's safety concerns.

2. Suspect's access to the victim or whether the suspect is stalking or has stalked the victim.

3. Previous or existing relationship or friendship between the victim and the suspect, or the suspect and the victim's spouse, or victim's dependents. The existence

of children in common. The sharing (or prior sharing) of a common domicile.

     4. Whether the suspect (or the suspect's friends or family members) has destroyed victim's property; threatened or attacked the victim; or threatened, attempted, or

has a plan to harm or kill the victim or the victim's family members; or intimidated the victim to withdraw participation in the investigation or prosecution.

     5. Whether the suspect has threatened, attempted, or has a plan to commit suicide.

     6. Whether the suspect has used a weapon, threatened to use a weapon, or has access to a weapon that may be used against the victim.

     7. Whether the victim has sustained serious injury during the sexual assault incident.

     8. Whether the suspect has a history of law enforcement involvement regarding domestic abuse, assault, or other criminal behavior.

     9. Whether the victim has a civilian protective order or command has an MPO against the suspect, or there has been a violation of a civilian protective order or MPO by the suspect.

     10. History of drug or alcohol abuse by either the victim or the suspect.

     11. Whether the suspect exhibits erratic or obsessive behavior, rage, agitation, or instability.

     12. Whether the suspect is a flight risk.

TRAINING REQUIREMENTS

1. Management of Training Requirements

a. Commanders, supervisors, and managers at all levels shall be responsible for the effective implementation of the Sexual Assault Prevention and Response (SAPR) program.

b. Military and DoD civilian officials at each management level shall advocate a robust SAPR program and provide education and training that shall enable them to prevent and appropriately respond to incidents of sexual assault.

c. Data shall be collected according to the annual reporting requirements as promulgated by DoD and explained in enclosure (12) of this Instruction.

2. General Training Requirements

a. Sexual Assault Prevention and Response training shall individually address SAPR prevention and response in accordance with enclosure (3) of this Instruction. These SAPR training requirements shall apply to all Service members and DoD civilian personnel who supervise Service members.

(1) Dedicated SAPR training shall be developed to ensure comprehensive knowledge of the required key concepts identified in this enclosure.

(2) The SAPR training, at a minimum, shall incorporate adult learning theory, which includes interaction and group participation.

(3) Upon request, the Service Chiefs shall submit a copy of SAPR training programs or SAPR training elements to DoD via the Department of the Navy Sexual Assault Prevention and Response Office (DON-SAPRO) for evaluation of consistency and compliance with DoD SAPR training standards in this Instruction. The Service Chiefs will ensure subsequent correction of any discrepancies identified by DoD regarding SAPR policy and training standards.

b. Commanders and managers responsible for training shall require that all personnel (i.e., all Service members,

Department of the Navy (DON) civilian personnel who supervise
Service members, and others as directed) are trained and that
completion of training data is annotated. Commanders for
accession training will ensure all new accessions are trained
and that completion of training data is annotated.

    c. If responsible for facilitating the training of
civilians supervising Service members, the unit commander or
civilian director shall require all SAPR training requirements
in this enclosure are met. The unit commander or civilian
equivalent shall be accountable for requiring data collection
regarding the training.

    d. The required subject matter for the training shall be
appropriate to the Service member's grade and commensurate with
their level of responsibility, to include:

    (1) Defining what constitutes sexual assault. Utilizing
the term "sexual assault" as defined in enclosure (2).

    (2) Explaining why sexual assaults are crimes.

    (3) Defining the meaning of "consent" as defined in
enclosure (2).

    (4) Explaining offender accountability and Uniform Code
of Military Justice (UCMJ) violations.

    (5) Explaining the distinction between sexual harassment
and sexual assault and that both are unacceptable forms of
behavior even though they may have different penalties.
Emphasizing the distinction between civil and criminal actions.

    (6) Explaining available reporting options (Restricted
and Unrestricted), the advantages and limitations of each
option, the effect of independent investigations on Restricted
Reports (see enclosure (4)) and explaining Military Rule of
Evidence (MRE) 514.

    (7) Providing an awareness of the SAPR program (DoD and
Service) and command personnel roles and responsibilities,
including all available resources for victims on and off base.

(8) Identifying prevention strategies and behaviors that may reduce sexual assault, including bystander intervention, risk reduction, and obtaining affirmative consent.

(9) Discussing process change to ensure that all sexual assault response services are gender-responsive, culturally-competent, and recovery-oriented.

(10) Discussing expedited transfers and Military Protective Order (MPO) procedures.

(11) Providing information to victims when the alleged perpetrator is the commander or in the victim's chain of command, to go outside the chain of command to report the offense to other commanding officers or an Inspector General. Victims shall be informed that they can also seek assistance from a legal assistance attorney or the DoD Safe Helpline.

(12) Discussing document retention for sexual assault documents ("Victim Reporting Preference Statement" [DD Form 2910] and "DoD Sexual Assault Forensic Examination (SAFE) Report" [DD Form 2911]), to include retention in investigative records. Explaining why it is recommended that sexual assault victims retain sexual assault records for potential use in Veterans Administration (VA) benefits applications.

3. <u>DoD Personnel Training Requirements</u>. Refer to Military Service-specific training officers that maintain personnel training schedules.

   a. Accessions training shall occur upon initial entry.

      (1) Mirror the General Training Requirements above.

      (2) Provide scenario-based, real-life situations to demonstrate the entire cycle of prevention, reporting, response, and accountability procedures to new accessions to clarify the nature of sexual assault in the military environment.

   b. Annual training shall occur once a year and is mandatory for all Service members regardless of rank or occupation or specialty.

      (1) Mirror the General Training Requirements above.

(2) Explain the nature of sexual assault in the military environment using scenario-based, real-life situations to demonstrate the entire cycle of prevention, reporting, response, and accountability procedures.

(3) Deliver to Service members in a joint environment from their respective Military Services and incorporate adult learning theory.

c. Professional Military Education (PME) and Leadership Development Training (LDT).

(1) For all trainees, PME and LDT shall mirror the General Training Requirements above.

(2) For senior noncommissioned officers and commissioned officers, PME and LDT shall occur during developmental courses throughout the military career and include:

(a) Explanation and analysis of the SAPR program.

(b) Explanation and analysis of the necessity of immediate responses after a sexual assault has occurred to counteract and mitigate the long-term effects of violence. Long-term responses after sexual assault has occurred will address the lasting consequences of violence.

(c) Explanation of rape myths (see SAPR Toolkit on www.sapr.mil), facts, and trends pertaining to the military population.

(d) Explanation of the commander's and senior enlisted Service member's role in the SAPR program.

(e) Review of all items found in the commander's protocols for Unrestricted Reports of sexual assault. (See SAPR Toolkit on www.sapr.mil.)

(f) Explanation of what constitutes reprisal (see enclosure (2)) and procedures for reporting allegations of reprisal.

d. Pre-deployment training shall be provided.

(1) Mirror the General Training Requirements above.

(2) Explain risk reduction factors tailored to the deployment location.

(3) Provide a brief history of the specific foreign countries or areas anticipated for deployment, and the area's customs, mores, religious practices, and status of forces agreement. Explain cultural customs, mores, and religious practices of coalition partners.

(4) Identify the type of trained sexual assault responders who are available during the deployment (e.g., law enforcement personnel, legal personnel, Sexual Assault Response Coordinator (SARC), Sexual Assault Prevention and Response Victim Advocates (SAPR VAs), healthcare personnel, chaplains).

(5) Upon implementation of the DoD Sexual Assault Advocate Certification Program (D-SAACP), and unless previously credentialed, include completion of certification for SARCs and SAPR VAs.

e. Post-deployment reintegration training shall occur within 30 days of returning from deployment and:

(1) Commanders of re-deploying personnel will ensure training completion.

(2) Explain available counseling and medical services, reporting options, and eligibility benefits for Service members and the Reserve Component.

(3) Explain MRE 514. Explain that Reserve members not in active service at the time of the incident or at the time of the report can make a Restricted or Unrestricted report with the SARC or SAPR VA when on active duty and then be eligible to receive SAPR services.

f. Pre-command training shall occur prior to filling a command position.

(1) Mirror the General Training Requirements above.

(a) The personnel trained shall include all officers who are selected for command and the unit's senior enlisted Service member.

(b) The required subject matter for the training shall be appropriate to the level of responsibility and commensurate with level of command.

(2) Explain rape myths, facts, and trends.

(3) Provide awareness of the SAPR program and explain the commander's and senior enlisted Service member's role in executing their SAPR service program.

(4) Review all items found in the commander's protocols for Unrestricted Reports of sexual assault. (See SAPR Toolkit on www.sapr.mil.)

(5) Explain what constitutes reprisal (see enclosure (2)) and procedures for addressing reprisal allegations.

4. General/Flag Officer (G/FO) and Senior Executive Service (SES) Personnel Training Requirements. G/FO and SES personnel training shall occur at the initial executive level program training and annually thereafter. Mirror the General Training Requirements above.

a. The Military Service executive level management offices are responsible for tracking data collection regarding the training.

b. The required subject matter for the training shall be appropriate to the level of responsibility and commensurate with level of command.

5. Military Recruiters. Military recruiter training shall occur annually and mirror the General Training Requirements above.

6. Training for Civilians. Training is required for civilians who supervise Service members, for all civilians, and, if feasible, highly recommended for DON contractors. Training shall occur annually and mirror the General Training Requirements above.

7. <u>Responder Training Requirements</u>. To standardize services throughout the DoD, all DON sexual assault responders shall receive the same baseline training. These minimum training standards form the baseline on which the Military Services and specialized communities can build. First responders are composed of personnel in the following disciplines or positions: SARCs; SAPR VAs; healthcare personnel; DON law enforcement; Naval Criminal Investigative Service (NCIS); judge advocates; chaplains; firefighters and emergency medical technicians. Commanders and Victim Witness Assistance Program (VWAP) personnel can be first responders. Commanders receive their SAPR training separately.

   a. All responder training shall:

      (1) Be given in the form of initial and annual refresher training from their Military Service as above. Responder training is in addition to annual training.

      (2) Be developed for each responder functional area from each military service and shall:

         (a) Explain the different sexual assault response policies and critical issues.

            <u>1</u>. DoD SAPR policy, including the role of the SARC, SAPR VA, victim witness liaison, and Case Management Group (CMG).

            <u>2</u>. Military Service-specific policies.

            <u>3</u>. Unrestricted and Restricted Reporting as well as MRE 514.

            <u>4</u>. Exceptions to Restricted Reporting and limitations to use.

            <u>5</u>. Change in victim reporting preference election.

            <u>6</u>. Victim advocacy resources.

         (b) Explain the requirement that SARCs must respond in accordance with this Instruction.

(c) Describe local policies and procedures with regards to local resources, referrals, procedures for military and civilians as well as collaboration and knowledge of resources and referrals that can be utilized at that specific geographic location.

(d) Explain the range of victim responses to sexual assault to include:

<u>1</u>. Victimization process, including re-victimization and secondary victimization.

<u>2</u>. Counterintuitive behavior.

<u>3</u>. Impact of trauma on memory and recall.

<u>4</u>. Potential psychological consequences, including acute stress disorder and post-traumatic stress disorder.

(e) Explain deployment issues, including remote location assistance.

(f) Explain the possible outcomes of investigations of sexual assault.

(g) Explain the possible flow of a sexual assault investigation. (See flowchart in the SAPR Policy Toolkit, located at www.sapr.mil.)

(h) Be completed prior to deployment.

(i) Recommend, but not require, that SAPR training for responders include safety and self-care.

b. SARC training shall:

(1) Provide the training requirement described above for all responders.

(2) Be scenario-based and interactive. Provide for role play where a trainee SARC counsels a sexual assault victim and is critiqued by a credentialed SARC and/or an instructor.

(3) Explain roles and responsibilities and command relationships.

(4) Explain the different reporting options, to include the effects of independent investigations (see enclosure (4) of this Instruction). Explain the exceptions to Restricted Reporting, with special emphasis on suspending Restricted Reporting where it is necessary to prevent or mitigate a serious and imminent threat to the health or safety of the victim or another person.

(5) Provide training on entering reports of sexual assault into Defense Sexual Assault Incident Database (DSAID) through interface with a Military Service data system or by direct data entry. Provide training on potential discovery obligations regarding any notes entered in DSAID.

(6) Provide training on document retention of Restricted and Unrestricted cases.

(7) Provide training on expedited transfer and MPO procedures.

(8) Provide instruction on all details of SAPR VA screening, including:

(a) What to do if SAPR VA is a recent victim, or knows sexual assault victims.

(b) What to do if SAPR VA was accused of being an offender or knows someone who was accused.

(c) Identifying the SAPR VA's personal biases.

(d) The necessary case management skills:

<u>1</u>. Required reports and proper documentation as well as records management.

<u>2</u>. Instruction to complete DD Form 2910 and proper storage according to Federal service privacy regulations.

<u>3</u>. Ability to conduct SAPR training, when requested by the SARC or commander.

        4. Transferring cases to another installation SARC.

(9) Explain the roles and responsibilities of the VWAP and the "Initial Information for Victims and Witnesses of Crime" form (DD Form 2701).

(10) Inform SARCs of the existence of the SAPRO website at http://www.sapr.mil, and encourage its use for reference materials and general DoD-level SAPR information.

c. SAPR VA training shall:

(1) Provide the responder training requirements as above.

(2) Be scenario-based and interactive. Provide for role play where a trainee SAPR VA counsels a sexual assault victim, and then that counseling session is critiqued by an instructor.

(3) Explain the different reporting options, to include the effects of independent investigations (see enclosure (4)). Explain the exceptions to Restricted Reporting, with special emphasis on suspending Restricted Reporting where it is necessary to prevent or lessen a serious and imminent threat to the health or safety of the victim or another person.

(4) Include:

(a) Necessary critical advocacy skills.

(b) Basic interpersonal and assessment skills.

        1. Appropriate relationship and rapport building.

        2. Sensitivity training to prevent re-victimization.

(c) Crisis intervention.

(d) Restricted and Unrestricted Reporting options as well as MRE 514.

(e) Roles and limitations, to include: command relationship, SAPR VA's rights and responsibilities, reporting to the SARC, and recognizing personal biases and issues.

(f) Preparing proper documentation for a report of sexual assault.

(g) Document retention in Restricted and Unrestricted cases.

(h) Expedited transfer and MPO procedures.

(i) Record keeping rules for protected disclosures relating to a sexual assault.

(j) A discussion of ethical issues when working with sexual assault victims as a victim advocate.

(k) A discussion of individual versus system advocacy.

(l) A review of the military justice process and adverse administrative actions.

(m) Overview of criminal investigative process and military judicial requirements.

(n) A review of the issues in victimology.

1. Types of assault.

2. Health consequences such as mental and physical health.

3. Cultural and religious differences.

4. Victims' rights and the victim's role in holding offenders appropriately accountable and limitations on offender accountability when the victim elects Restricted Reporting.

5. Healthcare management of sexual assault and medical resources and treatment options to include the medical examination, the forensic examination, mental health and

counseling, pregnancy, and Sexually Transmitted
Disease/Infection (STD/I) and Human Immunodeficiency Virus
(HIV).

     <u>6</u>. Identification of safety issues and their
immediate report to the SARC or law enforcement, as appropriate.

     <u>7</u>. Identification of reprisal and retaliation
actions against the victim; procedures for responding to
reprisal actions and their immediate reporting to the SARC and
the VWAP; safety planning to include how to prevent retaliation
or reprisal actions against the victim.

     <u>8</u>. Separation of the victim and offender as
well as the MPO and CPO process.

     <u>9</u>. Expedited transfer process for the victim.

     (o) An explanation of the roles and responsibilities
of the VWAP and DD Form 2701.

     (p) Safety and self-care, to include vicarious
trauma.

  d. Healthcare personnel training shall be in two distinct
training categories:

    (1) Training for Healthcare Personnel Assigned to a
Medical Treatment Facility (MTF). In addition to the responder
training requirements above, MTF healthcare personnel shall be
trained and remain proficient in medical treatment resources, in
conducting sexual assault patient interviews, and in conducting
the Sexual Assault Forensic Exam (SAFE) Kit process. Healthcare
personnel who receive a Restricted Report shall immediately call
a SARC or SAPR VA, so a DD Form 2910 can be completed.

    (2) Training for Healthcare Providers Performing SAFEs
in MTFs. In addition to the responder training requirements
above, healthcare providers performing SAFEs shall be trained
and remain proficient in conducting SAFEs. Healthcare providers
who may be called on to provide comprehensive medical treatment
to a sexual assault victim, including performing SAFEs are:
obstetricians and gynecologists and other licensed practitioners
(preferably family physicians, emergency medicine physicians,

and pediatricians); advanced practice nurses with specialties in midwifery, women's health, family health, and pediatrics; physician assistants trained in family practice or women's health; and registered nurses with documented education, training, and clinical practice in sexual assault examinations in accordance with reference (d). Healthcare personnel who receive a Restricted Report shall immediately call a SARC or SAPR VA so a DD Form 2910 can be completed.

(3) Healthcare personnel and provider training shall:

(a) Explain how to conduct a sexual assault patient interview to obtain medical history and assault information.

(b) Explain how to conduct a SAFE in accordance with reference (d) and include explanations on:

<u>1</u>. SAFE Kit and DD Form 2911.

<u>2</u>. Toxicology kit for suspected alcohol or drug-facilitated cases.

<u>3</u>. Chain of custody.

<u>4</u>. Translation of findings.

<u>5</u>. Proper documentation.

<u>6</u>. Storage of evidence in Restricted Reports (e.g., Restricted Report Case Number (RRCN)).

<u>7</u>. Management of the alleged offender.

<u>8</u>. Relevant local and State laws and restrictions.

<u>9</u>. Medical treatment issues during deployments including remote location assistance to include: location resources including appropriate personnel, supplies (drying device, toluidine blue dye, colposcope, camera), standard operating procedures, location of SAFE Kit and DD Form 2911; and availability and timeliness of evacuation to echelon of care where SAFEs are available.

(c) Explain how to deal with emergency contraception and STD/I treatment.

(d) Discuss physical and mental health assessment.

(e) Explain how to deal with trauma, to include:

<u>1</u>. Types of injury.

<u>2</u>. Photography of injuries.

<u>3</u>. Behavioral health and counseling needs.

<u>4</u>. Consulting and referral process.

<u>5</u>. Appropriate follow-up.

<u>6</u>. Drug or alcohol-facilitated sexual assault, to include review of best practices, victim interview techniques, and targeted evidence collections.

(f) Explain medical record management.

(g) Explain legal process and expert witness testimony.

e. Law enforcement (including NCIS) personnel, authorized to investigate violations of the UCMJ, training shall:

(1) Include the responder training requirements (above) for law enforcement personnel who may respond to a sexual assault complaint.

(2) Remain consistent with the guidelines published under the authority and oversight of the DoD Inspector General (IG). In addition, law enforcement training shall:

(a) Explain how to respond in accordance with the SAPR program.

<u>1</u>. Notify the command, SARC, and SAPR VA.

<u>2</u>. Work with SAPR VAs and SARCs, and medical personnel.

(b) Explain how to work with sexual assault victims, to include the effects of trauma on sexual assault victims. Ensure victims are informed of and accorded their rights by contacting the VWAP.

(c) Take into consideration the victim's safety concerns and medical needs.

(d) Review IG policy and applicable Service guidance regarding the legal transfer of the SAFE Kit and the retention of the DD Form 2911 or reports from civilian sexual assault forensic exams in archived files.

(e) Discuss sex offender issues.

f. Training for NCIS agents assigned to investigate sexual assaults shall:

(1) Be detailed in DoD IG policy.

(2) Adhere to the responder training requirements (above) for military and civilian criminal investigators assigned to NCIS who may respond to a sexual assault complaint.

(3) Remain consistent with the guidelines published under the authority and oversight of the DoD IG. In addition, NCIS training shall:

(a) Include initial and annual refresher training on essential tasks specific to investigating sexual assault investigations that explain that these reports shall be included in sexual assault quarterly and annual reporting requirements found in enclosure (12).

(b) Include DoD IG policy and Military Service regulations regarding the legal transfer of the SAFE Kit and the retention of the DD Form 2911 or reports from civilian sexual assault forensic exams in archived files.

(c) Explain how to work with victims of sexual assault.

<u>1</u>. Effects of trauma on the victim to include impact of trauma and stress on memory as well as balancing investigative priorities with victim needs.

<u>2</u>. Ensure victims are informed of and accorded their rights by contacting the VWAP.

<u>3</u>. Take into consideration the victim's safety concerns and medical needs.

(d) Explain how to respond to a sexual assault and the assigned Military Service regulations on:

<u>1</u>. Notification to command, SARC, and VWAP.

<u>2</u>. Investigating difficult cases to include drug and alcohol facilitated sexual assaults, having multiple suspects and sexual assaults in the domestic violence context as well as same-sex sexual assaults (male/male or female/female).

(e) Review of available research regarding false information and the factors influencing false reports and false information, to include possible victim harassment and intimidation.

(f) Explain unique issues with sex offenders to include identifying, investigating, and documenting predatory behaviors.

(g) Explain how to work with the SARC and SAPR VA to include SAPR VA and SARC roles, responsibilities, and limitations; victim services and support program; and MRE 514.

g. Judge advocate training shall:

(1) Prior to performing judge advocate duties, adhere to the responder training requirements (above) for judge advocates who are responsible for advising commanders on the investigation or disposition of, or who prosecute or defend, sexual assault cases.

(2) Explain legal support services available to victims.

(a) Pursuant to the Manual of the Judge Advocate General (JAGMAN) and respective Navy and Marine Corps regulations, explain that each Service member who reports a sexual assault shall be given the opportunity to consult with legal assistance counsel, and in cases where the victim may have been involved in collateral misconduct, to consult with defense counsel.

1. Provide information concerning the prosecution, if applicable, in accordance with reference (n). Provide information regarding the opportunity to consult with legal assistance counsel as soon as the victim seeks assistance from a SARC, SAPR VA, or any DoD law enforcement agent or judge advocate.

2. Ensure victims are informed of their rights and the VWAP program.

(b) Explain the sex offender registration program.

(3) Explain issues encountered in the prosecution and defense of sexual assaults, including updates to the Uniform Code of Military Justice, Manual for Courts Martial, and policies that impact the reporting, investigation, and disposition of sexual assault allegations.

(a) Victims' rights during trial and defense counsel interviews (e.g., guidance regarding answering questions on prior sexual behavior, interviewing parameters, coordinating interviews, case outcomes).

(b) In the case of a general or special court-martial involving a sexual assault (as defined in enclosure (2)), the right of a victim who testified to receive a copy of the prepared record of the proceedings of the court-martial (not to include sealed materials, unless otherwise approved by the presiding military judge or appellate court).

(c) Guidance on victim accompaniment (e.g., who may accompany victims to attorney interviews, what is their role, and what should they do if victim is being mistreated).

(d) MRE 412, 502, 513, and 514 directly applicable to victims of sexual assault.

(e) Protecting victim privacy (e.g., access to medical records and conversations with SARC or SAPR VA, discovery consequences of making victim's mental health an issue, MRE 514).

h. Legal assistance attorney training shall adhere to the requirements of annual training above. Attorneys shall receive training in order to have the capability to provide legal assistance to sexual assault victims. Legal assistance attorney training shall include:

(1) The VWAP, including the rights and benefits afforded the victim.

(a) The role of the VWAP and what privileges do or do not exist between the victim and the advocate or liaison.

(b) The nature of the communication made to the VWAP as opposed to those made to the legal assistance attorney.

(2) The differences between the two types of reporting in sexual assault cases.

(3) The military justice system, including the roles and responsibilities of the trial counsel, the defense counsel, and investigators. This may include the ability of the Government to compel cooperation and testimony.

(4) The services available from appropriate agencies or offices for emotional and mental health counseling and other medical services.

(5) The availability of protections offered by military and civilian restraining orders.

(6) Eligibility for and benefits potentially available as part of transitional compensation benefits, and other State and Federal victims' compensation programs.

(7) Traditional forms of legal assistance.

i. Chaplains and Religious Program Specialists (RPs) training shall:

(1) Adhere to the responder training requirements above.

(2) Pre-deployment SAPR training shall focus on counseling services needed by sexual assault victims and offenders in contingency and remote areas.

(3) Address:

(a) Privileged communications and the Restricted Reporting policy rules and limitations, including legal protections for chaplains and their confidential communications, assessing victim or offender safety issues (while maintaining chaplain's confidentiality), and MRE 514.

(b) How to support victims with discussion on sensitivity of chaplains in addressing and supporting sexual assault victims, identifying chaplain's own bias and ethical issues, trauma training with pastoral applications, and how to understand victims' rights.

(c) Other counseling and support topics.

<u>1</u>. Offender counseling should include: assessing and addressing victim and offender safety issues while maintaining confidentiality; and counseling an offender when the victim is known to the chaplain (counseling both the offender and the victim, when there is only one chaplain at a military installation).

<u>2</u>. Potential distress experienced by witnesses and bystanders over the assault they witnessed or about which they heard.

<u>3</u>. Counseling for SARCs, SAPR VAs, healthcare personnel, chaplains, JAGs, law enforcement or any other professionals, who routinely work with sexual assault victims and may experience secondary effects of trauma.

<u>4</u>. Providing guidance to unit members and leadership on how to mitigate the impact that sexual assault has on a unit and its individuals, while keeping in mind the needs and concerns of the victim.

DEFENSE SEXUAL ASSAULT INCIDENT DATABASE

1. Purpose

    a. The Defense Sexual Assault Incident Database (DSAID) supports DoD, Department of the Navy (DON), and Military Service SAPR program management and oversight activities. It shall serve as a centralized, case-level database for the collection and maintenance of information regarding sexual assaults involving persons covered by this Instruction. DSAID will include information, if available, about the nature of the assault, the victim, services offered to the victim, the offender, and the disposition of the reports associated with the assault. DSAID will serve as the DoD's Sexual Assault Prevention and Response (SAPR) source for internal and external requests for statistical data on sexual assault. DSAID has been assigned Office of Management and Budget control number 0704-0482. DSAID contains information provided by the military services, which are the original sources of the information.

    b. Disclosure of data stored in DSAID will only be granted when disclosure is authorized or required by law or regulation.

2. Procedures. DSAID shall:

    a. Contain information about sexual assaults reported to the DoD involving persons covered by this Instruction, both via Unrestricted and Restricted Reporting options.

    b. Include adequate safeguards to shield Personally Identifiable Information (PII) from unauthorized disclosure. The system will not contain PII about victims who make a Restricted Report. Information about sexual assault victims and subjects will receive the maximum protection allowed under the law. DSAID will include stringent user access controls.

    c. Assist with annual and quarterly reporting requirements, identifying and managing trends, analyzing risk factors or problematic circumstances, and taking action or making plans to eliminate or to mitigate risks. DSAID shall store case information. Closed case information shall be available to Department of Defense Sexual Assault Prevention and Response Office (DoD-SAPRO) for SAPR program oversight, study, research, and analysis purposes. DSAID will provide a set of core functions to satisfy the data collection and analysis requirements for the system in five basic areas: data warehousing, data query and reporting, Sexual Assault Response Coordinator (SARC) victim case management functions, subject investigative and legal case information, and SAPR program administration and management.

    d. Receive information from the Military Services' existing data systems or direct data entry by authorized Military Service personnel.

3. <u>Notification Procedure and Record Access Procedures</u>

    a. Requests for information contained in DSAID are answered by the Services. All requests for information should be made to the DoD Component that generated the information in DSAID. Individuals seeking to determine whether information about themselves is contained in this system of records or seeking access to records about themselves should address written inquiries to the appropriate Service office (see links to each Service webpage at <u>www.sapr.mil</u>).

    b. Responses to requests for information to the DoD Components must be responded to by the office(s) designated by the Component to respond to Freedom of Information Act (FOIA) (reference (o)) and Privacy Act (reference (p)) requests. Requests shall not be informally handled by the SARCs.

SEXUAL ASSAULT ANNUAL AND QUARTERLY REPORTING REQUIREMENTS

1. <u>Annual Reporting for the Military Services</u>. The Under Secretary of Defense for Personnel and Readiness (USD (P&R)) submits annual Fiscal Year (FY) reports to Congress on sexual assaults involving members of the Military Services. In coordination with the Department of the Navy Sexual Assault Prevention and Response Office (DON-SAPRO), the Navy and Marine Corps shall provide separate reports for the prior fiscal year on a schedule, determined by DON-SAPRO, that allows sufficient time for review by the Secretary of the Navy (SECNAV) and forwarding to the Secretary of Defense (SECDEF), through the Department of Defense Sexual Assault Prevention and Response Office (DoD-SAPRO), by March 1 of each year. Service inputs to the annual report shall include:

a. The policies, procedures, and processes in place or implemented by the Service-level Sexual Assault Prevention and Response (SAPR) program during the report year in response to incidents of sexual assault.

b. An assessment of the implementation of the policies and procedures on the prevention, response, and oversight of sexual assaults in the military to determine the effectiveness of SAPR policies and programs, including an assessment of how Service-level efforts executed Department of Defense (DoD) SAPR priorities.

c. Any plans for the following year on the prevention of and response to sexual assault, specifically in the areas of advocacy, healthcare provider and medical response, mental health, counseling, investigative services, legal services, and chaplain response.

d. Matrices for Restricted and Unrestricted Reports of the number of sexual assaults involving Service members, that includes case synopses, and disciplinary actions taken in substantiated cases and relevant information. (See the Appendix to this enclosure.)

e. Analyses of the matrices of the number of sexual assaults involving Service members.

2. <u>Quarterly Reports</u>. The quarterly data reports from the Military Services are the basis for annual reports, including the data fields necessary for comprehensive reporting. The information collected to prepare the quarterly reports has been assigned Report Control Symbol DD-P&R(A)2205. In quarterly reports, the policies and planned actions are not required to be reported. Each quarterly report and subsequent FY annual report shall update the status of those previously reported investigations that had been reported as opened but not yet completed or with action pending at the end of a prior reporting period. This reporting system will enable the DoD to track sexual assault cases from date of initiation to completion of command action or disposition. In coordination with DON-SAPRO, the Navy and Marine Corps shall provide separate quarterly reports on a schedule, determined by DON-SAPRO, that allows sufficient time for review and forwarding to DoD-SAPRO by the following dates:

a. February 15 for investigations opened during the period of October 1 - December 31.

b. May 15 for investigations opened during the period of January 1 - March 31.

c. August 15 for investigations opened during the period of April 1 - June 30.

d. The final quarterly report (July 1 - September 30) shall be included as part of the FY annual report.

3. <u>Annual Reporting for the United States Naval Academy (USNA)</u>. The USD (P&R) submits annual reports on sexual harassment and violence at USNA and the other Military Service Academies (MSAs) to the House of Representatives and Senate Armed Services Committees for each Academic Program Year (APY). The MSA Sexual Assault Survey conducted by the Defense Manpower Data Center (DMDC) has been assigned Report Control Symbol DD-P&R(A)2198.

a. In odd-numbered APYs, the Superintendent of USNA shall submit a report via DON-SAPRO to SECNAV assessing USNA policies, training, and procedures on sexual harassment and violence involving Midshipmen. The report shall be submitted according to a schedule, determined by DON-SAPRO, that allows sufficient time for review by SECNAV and forwarding to SECDEF no later than

October 15 of the following APY. The DMDC will simultaneously conduct gender relations surveys of Cadets and Midshipmen to collect information relating to sexual assault and sexual harassment at the MSAs to supplement these reports. DoD-SAPRO will summarize and consolidate the results of each MSA's APY assessment, which will serve as the mandated DoD annual report to Congress.

b. In even-numbered APYs, DoD-SAPRO and the DoD Diversity Management and Equal Opportunity (DMEO) Office conduct MSA site visits and a data call to assess each MSA's policies; training, and procedures regarding sexual harassment and violence involving Cadets and Midshipmen; perceptions of Academy personnel regarding program effectiveness; the number of reports and corresponding case dispositions; program accomplishments; progress made; and challenges. Together with the DoD-SAPRO and DMEO MSA visits, DMDC will conduct focus groups with Cadets and Midshipmen to collect information relating to sexual harassment and violence from the MSAs to supplement this assessment. DoD-SAPRO consolidates the assessments and focus group results of each MSA into a report, which serves as the mandated DoD annual report to Congress that will be submitted in December of the following APY. The Superintendent of USNA shall submit any data call inputs to DoD-SAPRO via DON-SAPRO according to a schedule determined by DON-SAPRO that allows sufficient time for review.

4. <u>Annual Reporting of Installation Data</u>. Installation data is drawn from the annual reports of sexual assault described above. In coordination with DON-SAPRO, the Navy and Marine Corps shall provide separate reports for the prior fiscal year, organized by installation, on a schedule, determined by DON-SAPRO, that allows sufficient time for review by SECNAV and forwarding to SECDEF, through DoD-SAPRO, by April 30 of each year. Reports shall contain matrices for Restricted and Unrestricted Reports of the number of sexual assaults involving Service members organized by military installation, and matrices including the synopsis and disciplinary actions taken in substantiated cases.

APPENDIX TO ENCLOSURE (12)
SEXUAL ASSAULT OFFENSE – DISPOSITION OF SUBJECTS IN SEXUAL
ASSAULT INVESTIGATIONS

Pursuant to legislated requirements, the following terms shall be used by the Services for annual and quarterly reporting of the dispositions of subjects in sexual assault investigations conducted by Naval Criminal Investigative Service (NCIS) or other Military Criminal Investigative Organizations (MCIOs). Services shall adapt their investigative policies and procedures, and their command and judicial actions, to comply with these terms.

    a. <u>Substantiated Reports</u>. Dispositions in this category come from Unrestricted Reports that have been investigated and found to have sufficient evidence to provide to command for consideration of action to take some form of punitive, corrective, or discharge action against an offender.

    (1) <u>Substantiated Reports Against Service Member Subjects</u>. A substantiated report of sexual assault is an Unrestricted Report that was investigated by an MCIO, provided to the appropriate military command for consideration of action, and found to have sufficient evidence to support the command's action against the subject. Actions against the subject may include initiation of a court-martial, non-judicial punishment, administrative discharge, and other adverse administrative action that result from a report of sexual assault or associated misconduct (e.g., adultery, housebreaking, and false official statement).

    (2) <u>Substantiated Reports by Service Member Victims</u>. A substantiated report of a sexual assault victim's Unrestricted Report that was investigated by an MCIO, and provided to the appropriate military command for consideration of action, and found to have sufficient evidence to support the command's action against the subject. However, there are instances where an Unrestricted Report of sexual assault by a Service member victim may be substantiated but the command is not able to take action against the person who is the subject of the investigation. These categories include the following: the subject of the investigation could not be identified; the subject died or deserted from the Service before action could be taken; the subject was a civilian or foreign national not

subject to the Uniform Code of Military Justice (UCMJ); or the subject was a Service member being prosecuted by a civilian or foreign authority.

b. <u>Substantiated Report Disposition Descriptions</u>. In the event of several types of action a commander takes against the same offender, only the most serious action taken is reported, as provided for in the following list, in descending order of seriousness. For each offender, any court-martial sentence and non-judicial punishment administered by commanders pursuant to Article 15 of the UCMJ is reported annually to the Department of Defense (DoD) in the case synopses or via the Defense Sexual Assault Incident Database (DSAID). Further additional actions of a less serious nature in the descending list should also be included in the case synopses reported to the Department. The number of victims associated with each of the following disposition categories shall be reported.

(1) <u>Commander Action for Sexual Assault Offense</u>.

(a) Court-Martial Charges Preferred (Initiated) for Sexual Assault Offense. A court-martial charge was preferred (initiated) for at least one of the offenses punishable by Articles 120 and 125 of the UCMJ, or an attempt to commit an Article 120 or 125, UCMJ offense that would be charged as a violation of Article 80 of the UCMJ.

(b) Non-judicial Punishments (Article 15, UCMJ). Disciplinary action for at least one of the UCMJ offenses comprised within the SAPR definition of sexual assault that was initiated pursuant to Article 15 of the UCMJ.

(c) Administrative Discharges. Commander action taken to involuntarily separate the offender from military service that is based in whole or in part on an offense within the SAPR definition of sexual assault.

(d) Other Adverse Administrative Actions. In the absence of an administrative discharge action, any other administrative action that was initiated (including corrective measures such as counseling, admonition, reprimand, exhortation, disapproval, criticism, censure, reproach, rebuke, extra military instruction, or other administrative withholding of privileges, or any combination thereof), and that is based in whole or in part on an offense within the Sexual Assault Prevention and Response (SAPR) definition of sexual assault. Cases should be placed in this category only when an administrative action other than an administrative discharge is the only action taken. If an "other administrative action" is taken in combination with another more serious action (e.g., courts-martial, non-judicial punishment, administrative discharge, or civilian or foreign court action), only report the case according to the more serious action taken.

        (2) <u>Commander Action for Other Criminal Offense</u>. Report actions against subjects in this category when there is probable cause for an offense, but only for a non-sexual assault offense (i.e., the commander took action on a non-sexual assault offense because an investigation showed that the allegations did not meet the required elements of, or there was insufficient evidence for, any of the UCMJ offenses that constitute the SAPR definition of sexual assault). Instead, an investigation disclosed other offenses arising from the sexual assault allegation or incident that met the required elements of, and there was sufficient evidence for, another offense under the UCMJ. Report court-martial charges preferred, non-judicial punishments, and sentences imposed in the case synopses provided to the DoD. The number of victims associated with each of the following disposition categories shall be reported.

        (a) Court-martial charges preferred (initiated) for a non-sexual assault offense.

        (b) Non-judicial punishments (Article 15, UCMJ) for non-sexual assault offense.

        (c) Administrative discharges for non-sexual assault offense.

        (d) Other adverse administrative actions for non-sexual assault offense.

   c. <u>Command Action Precluded</u>. Dispositions reported in this category come from an Unrestricted Report that was investigated by an MCIO and provided to the appropriate military command for consideration of action, but the evidence did not support taking action against the subject of the investigation because the victim declined to participate in the military justice action, there was insufficient evidence of any offense to take command action, the report was unfounded by command, the victim died prior to completion of the military justice action, or the statute of limitations for the alleged offense(s) expired. The number of victims associated with each of the following categories shall be reported.

      (1) <u>Victim Declined to Participate in the Military Justice Action</u>. Commander action is precluded or declined because the victim has declined to further cooperate with military authorities or prosecutors in a military justice action.

      (2) <u>Insufficient Evidence for Prosecution</u>. Although the allegations made against the alleged offender meet the required elements of at least one criminal offense listed in the SAPR definition of sexual assault (see enclosure (2)), there was insufficient evidence to legally prove those elements beyond a reasonable doubt and proceed with the case. (If the reason for concluding that there is insufficient evidence is that the victim declined to cooperate, then the reason for being unable to take action should be entered as "victim declined to participate in the military justice action," and not entered as "insufficient evidence.")

      (3) <u>Victim's Death</u>. Victim died before completion of the military justice action.

      (4) <u>Statute of Limitations Expired</u>. Determination that, pursuant to Article 43 of the UCMJ, the applicable statute of limitations has expired and the case may not be prosecuted.

  d. <u>Command Action Declined</u>. Dispositions in this category come from an Unrestricted Report that was investigated by an MCIO and provided to the appropriate military command for consideration of action, but the commander determined the report was unfounded as to the allegations against the subject of the investigation. Unfounded allegations reflect a determination by command, with the supporting advice of a qualified legal officer, that the allegations made against the alleged offender did not occur nor were attempted. These cases are either false or baseless. The number of victims associated with each of the following categories shall be reported.

(1) <u>False Cases</u>. Evidence obtained through an investigation shows that an offense was not committed nor attempted by the subject of the investigation.

(2) <u>Baseless Cases</u>. Evidence obtained through an investigation shows that alleged offense did not meet at least one of the required elements of a UCMJ offense constituting the SAPR definition of sexual assault or was improperly reported as a sexual assault.

e. <u>Subject Outside DoD's Legal Authority</u>. When the subject of the investigation or the action being taken are beyond DoD's jurisdictional authority or ability to act, use the following descriptions to report case disposition. Services shall also identify the number of victims associated with these dispositions and specify when there was insufficient evidence that an offense occurred in the following categories.

(1) <u>Offender is Unknown</u>. The investigation is closed because no person could be identified as the alleged offender.

(2) <u>Subject is a Civilian or Foreign National not Subject to UCMJ</u>. The subject of the investigation is not amenable to military UCMJ jurisdiction for action or disposition.

(3) <u>Civilian or Foreign Authority is Prosecuting Service Member</u>. A civilian or foreign authority has the sexual assault allegation for action or disposition, even though the alleged offender is also subject to the UCMJ.

(4) <u>Offender Died or Deserted</u>. Commander action is precluded because of the death or desertion of the alleged offender or subject of the investigation.

f. <u>Report Unfounded by MCIO</u>. Determination by the MCIO that the allegations made against the alleged offender did not occur nor were attempted. These cases are either false or baseless. The number of victims associated with this category shall be reported.

(1) <u>False Cases</u>. Evidence obtained through an MCIO investigation shows that an offense was not committed nor attempted by the subject of the investigation.

(2) <u>Baseless Cases</u>. Evidence obtained through an investigation shows that alleged offense did not meet at least one of the required elements of a UCMJ offense constituting the SAPR definition of sexual assault or was improperly reported as a sexual assault.